LET'S *talk*

DAVID CRYSTAL

LET'S talk

HOW ENGLISH CONVERSATION WORKS

OXFORD
UNIVERSITY PRESS

OXFORD
UNIVERSITY PRESS

Great Clarendon Street, Oxford, OX2 6DP,
United Kingdom

Oxford University Press is a department of the University of Oxford.
It furthers the University's objective of excellence in research, scholarship,
and education by publishing worldwide. Oxford is a registered trade mark of
Oxford University Press in the UK and in certain other countries

Published in the United States of America by Oxford University Press
198 Madison Avenue, New York, NY 10016, United States of America

British Library Cataloguing in Publication Data
Data available

Library of Congress Control Number: 2019948971

ISBN 978–0–19–885069–4

Printed and bound in Great Britain by
Clays Ltd, Elcograf S.p.A.

Contents

Preface

I first found myself transcribing and analysing conversation for Randolph Quirk's Survey of English Usage at University College London in 1962. A decade later, along with the assistant director of the Survey, Derek Davy, I made a set of recordings of everyday informal conversation from which extracts were selected for a book, *Advanced Conversational English* (Longman, 1975), written with the needs of teachers of English as a second language in mind, but now long out of print. I revisited these recordings as a primary source for the present book, and they can now be heard on my website: <http://www.davidcrystal.com>. It can be difficult getting a sense of the natural flow of conversations just from a transcription, so I do recommend listening to the examples I use, especially the one quoted in full in the Appendix. For more recent illustrations of conversation, and a wider range of speakers, I've used recordings available in modern corpora as well as clips from YouTube. These are listed in the references at the end of the book.

Innumerable writers have reflected on the nature of conversation over the centuries, and I've included many quotations from them, from Cicero onwards, to provide a kind of literary counterpoint to my linguistic description. I've made considerable use of the collection Hilary Crystal and I compiled for our anthology *Words on Words: Quotations about Language and Languages* (2000), especially the section on conversation—though supplemented by extracts from writing that has appeared since then. The first edition of *Words on Words* is another of my books that is now out of print, but a new text is available as an e-book or print-on-demand through my website (see references, p. 198).

David Crystal
Holyhead, 2019

Prologue

English has no shortage of words to describe conversations, and our manner of speaking, and no shortage of authors who have reflected on them. Some examples:

badinage, banter, blether, blurt, burble…

> Conversation is an art in which a man has all mankind for his competitors, for it is that which all are practising every day while they live. (Ralph Waldo Emerson, *The Conduct of Life*)

> The art of conversation is the art of hearing as well as of being heard. (William Hazlitt, *The Plain Speaker*)

…chaff, chat, chatter, chit-chat, chitter-chatter, confab…

> 'So, let me show you how a conversation works. I say something, and then you say something back that actually relates to what I was talking about, as if you were even the least bit interested.'

> 'Huh?' I say. (Jodi Picoult, *Between the Lines*)

> Whenever Percy stopped by to see her [Annabeth], she was so lost in thought that the conversation went something like this:
> Percy: 'Hey, how's it going?'
> Annabeth: 'Uh, no thanks.'
> Percy: 'Okay … have you eaten anything today?'
> Annabeth: 'I think Leo is on duty. Ask him.'
> Percy: 'So, my hair is on fire.'
> Annabeth: 'Okay, in a while.' (Rick Riordan, *The Mark of Athena*)

…gab, gas, go on, gossip, gush…

> The whole force of conversation depends on how much you can take for granted. (Oliver Wendell Holmes, *The Autocrat of the Breakfast Table*)

> It does seem so pleasant to talk with an old acquaintance that knows what you know. I see so many of these new folks nowadays,

that seem to have neither past nor future. Conversation's got to have some root in the past, or else you've got to explain every remark you make, an' it wears a person out. (Sarah Orne Jewitt, *The Country of Pointed Firs*)

...harangue, heads-up, heart-to-heart, hint, hot air...

Galinda didn't often stop to consider whether she believed in what she said or not; the whole point of conversations was flow. (Gregory Maguire, *Wicked*)

Everybody talks, but there is no conversation. (Dejan Stojanovic, *The Sun Watches the Sun*)

...jabber, jaw, jeer, jest, joke, kid, mock...

Conversation is like playing tennis with a ball made of Krazy Putty that keeps coming back over the net in a different shape. (David Lodge, *Small World*)

Conversation should be like juggling; up go the balls and plates, up and over, in and out, good solid objects that glitter in the footlights and fall with a bang if you miss them. (Evelyn Waugh, *Brideshead Revisited*)

...natter, parley, pillow talk, powwow, prattle...

Conversation needs pauses, thoughts need time to make love. (Theodore Zeldin, *Conversation*)

...ramble, rant, rave, repartee, rib...

Conversation is never easy for the British, who are never keen to express themselves to strangers or, for that matter, anyone, even themselves. (Malcolm Bradbury, *Rates of Exchange*)

...small-talk, spout, table talk, tattle, tell-tale, tête-à-tête, yak, yap, yarn

What are the factors that motivate so many different kinds of talk? What are the rules that we use unconsciously, even in the most routine exchanges of everyday conversation? We think of conversation as something spontaneous, instinctive, habitual—'the most fruitful and natural play of the mind', as Montaigne put it in one of his essays. But there are rules—or, if that word is too strong, conventions, fashions, expectations. Conversation has been described as an art, as a game, sometimes even as a battle. Whichever metaphor we use, most people are unaware of what the rules are, how they work, and how we can bend and break them when circumstances warrant it. The analysis of conversation turns out to be one of the most fascinating in linguistic study for that very reason.

> When two Englishmen meet, their first talk is of the weather.
> (Dr Johnson, *The Idler*)

True enough...but first they must greet each other.

Chapter One

GREETINGS!

People are gathering for a meeting scheduled to start at 9 am. Andrew is the first to arrive, soon followed by Steve. *Good morning*, they say to each other. Nothing unusual about that.

In walks Emily. *Good morning*, she says to Andrew, and then *Good morning* to Steve. Then she does a double take, and says, *Oh sorry, I've already said good morning to you, haven't I*. It seems they met in the car park outside, and exchanged the first greeting of the day there.

Why does Emily feel the need to apologize?

A polite vocal greeting is the norm when people who are about to engage in some sort of interaction meet each other. It is of course possible to stay silent, but that would be very unusual. If Emily said nothing on her arrival, it would convey a negative attitude—some sort of private problem, perhaps, or a suppressed antagonism. The norm is to break the silence, to recognize each other with a brief verbal handshake. It's a mutual affirmation of identity, an acceptance by each that the other has a personal role to play in what is about to happen.

So if we're greeted a second time, it's as if that first encounter never happened. The double-greeted one might well feel: 'Was I so unimportant to you that you don't even remember meeting me a little while ago?' Sensitive double-greeters realize they've made a small social faux pas, so they rush to apologize for it.

It's a basic politeness rule in English: we don't say *good morning* to somebody more than once. And we are good at keeping a mental log of the people we meet so that we don't double-greet. It's a remarkable and totally unconscious skill.

But it only applies to greetings. It doesn't apply to farewells. Imagine now the end of the meeting. It has lasted all day, and as people leave they say *good night* to each other. Emily is almost the last to leave. She says *good night* to Steve and goes out. Then, having forgotten a bag, half a minute later she returns. Steve is still there. She picks up her bag, and leaves a second time. *Good night* she says to him again, and he does the same. Neither apologizes for saying *good night* a second time.

If you're learning to speak English, *good morning* and *good night* are two of the phrases you pick up early on, along with *good afternoon* and *good evening*. They seem 'the same'—and from the point of view of how they are grammatically constructed, they are. But from the point of view of pragmatics—how they are actually used in the language—they are some distance apart.

The same difference turns up in saying *hello* and *goodbye*. If we meet a friend at a railway station, we typically say *hello*—but just once. We don't repeat it as the person gets closer and closer to us. But when the friend is leaving, we can say *goodbye* emotionally several times. We can even shout it to each other repeatedly down the platform as the train is pulling out: *Bye...bye...bye...bye...*

Some exceptions

There *is* a situation where we might utter a greeting several times in succession: when we're being jovial. If Jane walks into an office with a *Good morning, good morning, good morning*, it shows she's in a good mood. If Fred arrives at a party, and greets everyone with a cheery *Hello, hello, hello!*, it's a way of announcing that he's there. People are more likely to take notice than if he used a single loud *Hello!* It also shows that he's ready to party.

Saying something three times is a common strategy of speech-makers when they want to make an impact:

On this day, in this election, at this defining moment, change has come to America. (Barack Obama, 2008)

Education, education, education—the top three priorities! (Tony Blair, 1997)

Of course there's no fixed limit: we could carry on repeating *hello* or *good evening* indefinitely, as Stephen Fry often did to camera when he was introducing the television series *QI*. In everyday interactions I've never heard it used more than five times in a row—and even with five, we would probably feel the speaker was overdoing it.

Another multi-*hello* situation is when we're melodramatically expressing a discovery. There are innumerable scenarios—a gardener coming across an unusual plant (with a surprised intonation), a scientist observing an unexpected result (with a meditative intonation), someone at a party encountering a pretty or handsome guest (with an admiring intonation). It's also the classic utterance of a policeman coming round a corner and encountering a suspicious activity: *'Allo, 'allo, 'allo*.

Again, it's usual to say it three times, though policemen—judging by film scripts (I have never been the actual recipient of such an utterance)—often make do with two. The intonation is distinctive: the opening *hello*(s) are low and flat, and the final one rises—ominously.

But, with the study of conversation, there are always exceptions to the exceptions. The other day I heard someone say *hello* a dozen times, each time in a loud breathy voice, with the two syllables given equal stress, and it didn't seem strange at all. The recipient? An excited dog, greeting its owner after a period of absence, tail wagging furiously. With each burst of canine energy, the owner responded with an animated *hello*.

Unusual sequences

Good morning is said in the morning; *good afternoon* in the afternoon; and *good night* at the end of the day—true? Not entirely.

'Good morning' in the afternoon
Jane has had a very long lie-in, after a very late night, and doesn't rise until 2. As she staggers downstairs, she is met by her flatmate with a lively (or sarcastic) *good morning*.

'Good afternoon' in the morning
David arrives late at the office. He should be there by 9, but traffic has held him up and he doesn't get to his desk until 10. He is greeted by a chorus of mocking *good afternoon*s from his colleagues—and perhaps by a sarcastic *good afternoon* from his boss.

'Good night' in the morning or afternoon
The party went on very late, but Peter has had to go to work as usual. As he sits at his desk, one of his wide-awake colleagues notices him dozing off, pats him on the back with a cheery *good night*, and thereby wakes him up.

It's not difficult to think of other scenarios that illustrate exceptions to the general rule, and the same applies to other greetings and farewells. The response to *hello* is *hello*, and the response to *goodbye* is *goodbye*—true? Again, not entirely.

'Hello' followed by 'goodbye'
Mary is in a hurry, leaving the office. As she rushes out of the front door she meets Arthur coming in. *Hello*, says Arthur. *Goodbye*, says Mary—perhaps adding an apology to avoid sounding too abrupt: *Sorry, got a train to catch...*

'Goodbye' followed by 'hello'
As seen in this Internet headline:

General election 2017: Goodbye and Hello—who has a seat?

Nick Clegg will be saying goodbye to Westminster, but who will be returning?...

'Good morning' followed by 'hello'
When people who know each other exchange an informal greeting, they often dispense with a symmetrical exchange. A *good morning*

may be acknowledged by a friendly *hello*, *hi*, or similar response. Or the other way round.

'Good morning' followed by no response

When a greeting is addressed to a group of people, a response is optional, and often inappropriate. Sitting in the departure lounge at St Pancras International, a businessman joined a group of five fellow travellers and greeted them with a cheery *good morning*. They all acknowledged his presence with their faces, but none of them replied with a vocal response. In another group nearby, a similar greeting attracted a corresponding *good morning* from just one member of the party—the others evidently accepting that this would suffice for all of them. In addressing a large group, such as a lecture audience, the lecturer's *good morning* would usually be considered to be no more than a piece of conventional politeness, and be received in silence. Indeed, it would be somewhat odd if someone in the back row were to shout out *good morning* in reply. On the other hand, in a church setting, a priest's *good morning, everyone* to the congregation received a sporadic chorus of *good morning, father* in reply. It seems that there is no general rule: rather, we need to observe the norms of a particular situation and decide whether we wish to follow them or not.

The 'good morning' scenarios illustrate an exchange restricted to a single *turn*: each person speaks once. They would never be described as conversations. As we'll see in the next chapters, to count as a conversation there needs to be more substance. But greetings do clearly display one of the basic notions in conversation analysis: the concept of *turn-taking*. A single contribution from a speaker is called a *conversational turn*. It's one of several metaphors that linguists use to capture the essence of shared talk. Another is the *conversational ball*: I hold the ball while I'm talking, and pass it to you when it's your turn, and then you pass it back to me—when the conversation is running smoothly, of course. (I'll talk about cases where it isn't later.) Neither metaphor is new. In the eighteenth century, Jonathan Swift was one who talked about the 'ball of discourse', and it is this historical perspective that I find especially illuminating as a way in to the investigation of conversations today.

I used the term *pragmatics* at the beginning of this chapter, and it's a perspective from this field in linguistics that will provide a frame of reference for much of this book. The name is an application of the everyday use of the word *pragmatic*. Someone who is pragmatic (according to the *Oxford English Dictionary*) deals 'with matters in accordance with practical rather than theoretical considerations or general principles; aiming at what is achievable rather than ideal; matter-of-fact, practical, down-to-earth'. There's an implication of adaptability—of altering our behaviour to suit the needs of a situation. It contrasts with *dogmatic*, where no such flexibility is tolerated.

The notion appealed to linguists because it tied in perfectly with the concept of *choice*—a notion that is central to language use, and a major focus of several linguists, such as Michael Halliday. We constantly make choices when using language—choosing one word rather than another, or one grammatical construction, pronunciation, or punctuation mark rather than another. We make stylistic choices, such as deciding whether to be formal or informal, and this will be a major factor in talking about conversation. Teachers are always dealing with choice when they correct the work of their students: a correction is an identification of a wrong choice on the part of the student. And later (in Chapter 16) we'll see cases of people who are unable to make appropriate linguistic choices because of some disability. My definition of pragmatics accordingly is: the study of the choices—appropriate or inappropriate—we make when we use language in different situations, the reasons for those choices, and the effects that those choices convey.

Good mornings

The series of examples in Chapter 1 illustrates a very important feature of conversation, especially in informal settings: its essentially creative and unpredictable character. There are clearly norms, conventions, and expectations, but it doesn't take much for people to find ways of departing from them for all sorts of reasons. We may wish to convey an atmosphere, build rapport, make an impact, create an effect, trigger a laugh... And our choice may be tacitly acknowledged, given a minimal response, or even become a talking point, as in Chapter 1 of J. R. R. Tolkien's *The Hobbit*, when Bilbo meets Gandalf:

> 'Good morning!' said Bilbo, and he meant it. The sun was shining, and the grass was very green. But Gandalf looked at him from under long bushy eyebrows that stuck out further than the brim of his shady hat.
>
> 'What do you mean?' he said. 'Do you wish me a good morning, or mean that it is a good morning whether I want it or not; or that you feel good this morning; or that it is a morning to be good on?'
>
> 'All of them at once,' said Bilbo. 'And a very fine morning for a pipe of tobacco out of doors, into the bargain.'

Gandalf tells Bilbo he is looking for someone to share in an adventure. He stays looking at Bilbo in silence. Bilbo tries to ignore him, until...

> 'Good morning!' he said at last. 'We don't want any adventures here, thank you! You might try over The Hill or across The Water.' By this he meant that the conversation was at an end.

'What a lot of things you do use *Good morning* for!' said Gandalf.
'Now you mean that you want to get rid of me, and that it won't be
good till I move off.'

And indeed, a *good morning* (or ... *afternoon/evening*) is often used as an
indication that a conversational encounter has come to an end, as
an alternative or supplement to other expressions of closure such
as *thank you* or *goodbye*. It may be no more than an optional vocal
'nod' of politeness, as when leaving a shop or restaurant, or passing
someone in the street. It may be abrupt and cold, as when Scrooge
(in the opening chapter of Charles Dickens' *A Christmas Carol*) uses
good afternoon four times to stop his nephew's enthusiastic flow,
ending in yet another unusual sequence:

'A merry Christmas, Uncle!'
'Good afternoon!' said Scrooge.
'And A Happy New Year!'
'Good afternoon!' said Scrooge.

At the close of an interview or audition, a *thank you* to the candidate
followed by a *goodbye* could suggest a greater degree of finality (we
don't expect to see you again, i.e. you haven't got the job) than a *thank
you* followed by a *good morning*. It isn't just Bilbo who uses *good morning* in a remarkable number of ways.

Chapter Two

IN THE BEGINNING . . .

In the beginning, talk had nothing to do with it. When the word *conversation* came into English from French in the fifteenth century, it meant living or being in a place or among people. A common reflection was to refer to one's future state in the next world: 'For our conversation is in heaven', says St Paul in Chapter 3 of his epistle to the people of Philippi (*King James Bible* translation, 1611). More modern versions would replace this by a different noun, such as *citizenship* or *homeland*. It was also a common way of referring to a circle of acquaintance, or one's place in society: in the first translation of *Don Quixote* in 1620 the good knight quotes a proverb: 'You may know the Man by the Conversation he keeps' (Book 6, Chapter 27). Today we would say *company*.

Conversation, then, chiefly referred to behaviour, to the way people conducted themselves in daily life. This is how Shakespeare uses the word, as when Enobarbus describes Octavia as someone 'of a holy, cold, and still conversation' (in *Antony and Cleopatra*, 2.6.121). And the notion of living or being together soon led to more intimate senses, including sexual ones. According to Richard, Duke of Gloucester, one of the reasons for the downfall of Hastings was 'his conversation with Shore's wife' (*Richard III*, 3.5.31). The legal concept of *crim con* ('criminal conversation') was a regular source of public scandal in the eighteenth century: this was an action that allowed a husband to obtain damages from the lover of his adulterous wife. (There was no similar action available for women.) The non-verbal nature of *conversation* in its early use is clearly shown in an observation by the sixteenth-century musician and theologian John Marbeck. A comment in his miscellany of commonplace thoughts (1581) reads: 'True pietie doth not consist in knowledge & talking, but in the action and conversation.'

The modern, vocal sense begins to emerge in the sixteenth century, with a first recorded use by Sir Philip Sidney in his prose romance *Arcadia* (1590). There's a clear vocal sense presented when Philoclea goes up to Pamela's chamber 'to joy her thoughts with the sweet conversation of her beloved sister' (Book 2, 145), and this was well established by the time Dr Johnson compiled his dictionary in 1755. His definition of *conversation* is 'a particular act of discoursing upon any subject'. What did people say before this vocal sense developed? How would they have said 'have a conversation' in Middle English? They would 'make a dialogue', 'have a speak', or 'have a speech'. And earlier, in Old English, they would simply 'have speech'. Bede in his *Ecclesiastical History* records how the kings Oswy and Egbert 'hæfdon betweoh him spræce' ['had between them conversation'] in order to decide what needed to be done about the state of the English Church.

We see the full flowering of the modern vocal sense in Jonathan Swift's *Polite Conversation* (1738)—in full, *A Complete Collection of genteel and ingenious Conversation, according to the most polite mode and method now used at Court, and in the best Companies of England.* This was entirely about social chit-chat: the author, one 'Simon Wagstaff Esq', records three dialogues—at breakfast, dinner, and tea—satirizing the banality of everyday social discourse, full of the formulaic greetings and leave-takings, the slang and catchphrases, the mild oaths and colloquialisms widely used in the early eighteenth century. His intention, he avers in his introduction, is to be helpful, having observed with much grief...

how frequently both Gentlemen, and Ladies, are at a Loss for Questions, Answers, Replies, and Rejoynders. However, my Concern was much abated, when I found, that these Defects were not occasioned by any Want of Materials, but because these Materials were not in every Hand. For Instance: One Lady can give an Answer better than ask a Question. One Gentleman is happy at a Reply; another excels in a Rejoynder: One can revive a languishing Conversation, by a sudden surprizing Sentence; another is more dextrous in seconding; a third can fill the Gap with laughing or commending what hath been said. Thus, fresh Hints may be started, and the Ball of Discourse kept up.

But alas, this is too seldom the Case, even in the most select Companies. How often do we see at Court, at publick visiting Days, at great Men's Levees [receptions], and other Places of general Meeting, that the Conversation falls and drops to nothing, like a Fire without supply of Fuel. This is what we all ought to lament; and against this dangerous Evil, I take upon me to affirm, that I have in the following Papers provided an infallible Remedy.

Here are the opening exchanges of his *Polite Conversation*: Lord Sparkish meets Colonel Atwit in St James's Park. (As is usual in eighteenth-century dialogue, proper names are italicized. I gloss the expressions that are obscure today.)

COLONEL. Well met, my Lord.

LORD SP. Thank ye, Colonel; a Parson would have said, I hope we shall meet in Heaven. When did you see *Tom. Neverout*?

COL. He's just coming towards us. Talk of the Devil. –

[*Neverout comes up.*]

COL. How do you do *Tom*?

NEV. Never the better for you. ['No better for your asking']

COL. I hope you're never the worse. But, where's your Manners? Don't you see my Lord *Sparkish*?

NEV. My Lord, I beg your Lordship's Pardon.

LORD SP. *Tom*, How is it? what, you can't see the Wood for Trees? What Wind blew you hither?

NEV. Why, my Lord, it is an ill Wind that blows no Body Good; for it gives me the Honour of seeing your Lordship.

COL. *Tom*, you must go with us to Lady *Smart's* to Breakfast.

NEV. Must! why Colonel. *Must* is for the King. ['Only kings have the right to be so peremptory']

[*Colonel offering in jest to draw his Sword.*]

COL. Have you spoke with all your Friends? ['asked them to support you in a duel']

NEV. Colonel, as you are stout, be merciful.

LORD SP. Come, agree, agree, the Law's costly.

[*Colonel taking his Hand from the Hilt.*]

NEV. What, do you think I was born in a Wood to be scar'd by an Owl? [proverbial: 'owls don't scare those who live near a wood']

COL. Well Tom, you are never the worse Man for being afraid of me. Come along.

NEV. I'll wait on you. I hope Miss *Notable* will be there. I gad [a gentle oath—'by God'] she's very handsome, and has Wit at Will. ['can be witty whenever she pleases']

COL. Why; every one as they like ['everyone to their liking']; as the good Woman said, when she kiss'd her Cow.

And they arrive at the house. The conversation continues in this vein for over 700 turns. Apart from the eighteenth-century idioms and some minor grammatical differences, the language of this repartee isn't very different from what we would hear today. There seems to be a core of conversational strategies that haven't changed—and not just since the eighteenth century, as we'll see in Chapter 3.

New contexts for conversation

The word *conversation* greatly extended its range during the eighteenth century. It came to be used to describe a regular social occasion (an 'at home') where people met to talk about things—what would later be called a *conversazione*. 'Lady Pomfret has a charming conversation once a week', writes Horace Walpole in his correspondence (1740). This didn't mean that her social talk was restricted to a single occasion.

In painting, a new genre evolved: the *conversation piece*, where we see a group of people informally engaged in talking to each other. They're usually seen in gardens, or in the countryside, or in elegant drawing rooms, as in 'The Marriage Settlement' (1745) by William Hogarth. A great deal of serious chat is clearly taking place. But conversations are not just the province of the upper classes. Hogarth portrayed a rather different kind of setting in his etching 'A Midnight Modern Conversation' (1733): a tavern drinking scene in which eleven men sit around a punchbowl in various stages of vocal inebriation. One is half asleep. Another has fallen over. A chamber pot overflows in the corner.

By the end of the century, and into the next, the notion of 'having a conversation' was so well established that fashionable society found it necessary to find new ways and means to facilitate it. *Conversation chairs* are described in Thomas Sheraton's *The Cabinet-maker and Upholsterer's Drawing-book* (1791):

> The conversation chairs are used in library or drawing-rooms. The parties who converse with each other sit with their legs across the seat, and rest their arms on the top rail, which, for this purpose, is made about three inches and an half wide, stuffed and covered.

Victorian furniture-makers developed the concept further: the two seats were joined but in opposite directions, so that the parties could easily turn to face each other over a shared rail. Some airline seats in business class are designed on the same principle.

Then, towards the end of the eighteenth century, there was a craze for *conversation cards*, on both sides of the Atlantic. An advertisement in the *Baltimore Daily Intelligencer* for 1794 read:

> A new and elegant Edition of the much admired Conversation Cards: Containing a variety of amusing, entertaining, and innocent *Questions & Answers* in the art of courtship. Each pack contains 64 cards.

Later, towards the end of the Victorian era, they developed into *flirtation cards* (also called *escort* or *acquaintance cards*). The card would have a simple message on it, such as *May I See You Home?*, or a more elegant, flowery, or cheeky invitation. Usually slipped surreptitiously by a man to a woman at a social gathering, there were also answer cards available to accept or deny the request. Some of the cards anticipated the chat abbreviations of Internet times. *MAY I. C. U. HOME?* reads one (p. 17). The practice died away during the early twentieth century. Today, of course, such invites would probably arrive as a text message.

Another popular development, towards the end of the Victorian era, was the *conversation sweet*—a small circular sweet with an embossed message, introduced by the Yorkshire firm of Joseph Dobson. At first called *conversation lozenges*, they contained a moral or romantic message, such as 'Take ye Not to Strong Drink' or 'Give Me Your Heart'. The New England firm of Necco had a similar range of candies in such shapes as hearts, baseballs, and horseshoes. The heart-shaped lozenges known as *sweethearts* soon achieved literary fame: we find them mentioned in Canadian author Lucy Maud Montgomery's *Anne of Green Gables* (1908), written soon after the candies were introduced:

> Once, when nobody was looking, Gilbert took from his desk a little pink candy heart with a gold motto on it, 'You are sweet', and slipped it under the curve of Anne's arm. Whereupon Anne arose, took the pink heart gingerly between the tips of her fingers, dropped it on the floor, ground it to powder beneath her heel, and resumed her position without deigning to bestow a glance on Gilbert.

A century later, the same principle motivated *Love Hearts* from Swizzel Matlow in the UK (the messages always in capital letters): *YOU'RE FAB, BE GOOD, LOVE YOU, BYE BYE, COOL DUDE, GUESS WHO*... A popular children's pastime is to take a handful and arrange them into messages for friends. There are adult equivalents, rather more risqué in character. The supermarket firm Asda in the UK has a range called *Whatevers* containing present-day catchphrases and slang, such as *BOTHERED, YOU WHAT?, RESPECT,* and *MINT.* In the USA a handful from a packet brought to light *AWE SOME, EMAIL ME, LOL,* and *URA QT.* The texting abbreviation craze must have been the answer to a prayer for the manufacturer's creatives, always keen to find new messages.

The word *conversation*, in its modern English sense, is only some 400 years old, but the phenomenon of conversing, one assumes, is going to be as old as the language itself. Is there any evidence?

Conversation cards

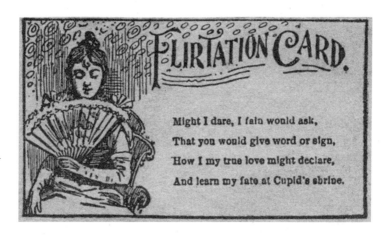

Conversation cards died away? Not entirely. In Part 4 of Monty Python's *The Meaning of Life* (1983), we see a waiter (John Cleese) in a restaurant coming up to a retired couple, Mr and Mrs Hendy (Eric Idle and Michael Palin), who are sitting opposite each other in an awkward silence:

WAITER: Good evening. Would you care for something to talk about? [*handing out menus*]

MR HENDY: Oh that would be wonderful.

WAITER: Our special tonight is minorities.

MR HENDY: Oh that sounds really interesting.

The couple eventually choose philosophy, and to help them get started he hands out conversation cue cards. The scene can be viewed on YouTube (see p. 198).

The process has a serious analogue in the popular 'conversation dinners', such as those hosted by the educational company The School of Life, founded by Alain de Botton in 2008. An envelope containing topics is by your place, and this starts a conversation off. There are also commercially available card decks that can be used to start conversations, going by such names as reflection cards, conversation starters, and conversation menus. Some firms classify them into subject areas or occasions, such as mealtimes, thanksgivings, Christmas, children's parties, and even funerals. It certainly beats jokes from Christmas crackers as a way of keeping a conversation going.

Chapter Three

A THOUSAND YEARS OF CONVERSATION

There is little sign of everyday conversation in the surviving manuscripts of Old English, spoken during a period of some 600 years after the arrival of the Anglo-Saxons in the fifth century. Formal words are sometimes exchanged between warriors, such as the heroes in *Beowulf* and in *The Battle of Maldon*, but these dialogues are highly crafted rhetorical verse. There are however two places where we can hear the sound of an ordinary conversation, and they both show that nothing much has changed between then and now.

The first is a fragment of talk recounted by the historian Bede in his Latin *Ecclesiastical History*, where he tells the story of a seventh-century illiterate cowherd, Cædmon (pronounced [<u>kad</u>-mun]), who became England's first Christian poet. In an Old English translation made some 200 years later, we read that he left a social evening, full of shame when it was his turn to sing, because he felt he couldn't, and fell asleep in his cattle-stall. A voice came to him in a dream, and called him by name. If we ignore the narrative verbs in the text ('he said', 'he answered'), the conversation went like this (in modern English translation):

VOICE: Cædmon, sing me something.
CÆDMON: I can't sing anything, and that is why I left the banquet
and came here, because I didn't know how to sing.

VOICE: But you can sing for me.
CÆDMON: What shall I sing?
VOICE: Sing me creation.

And he does, producing a 9-line poem about God the Creator known today as 'Cædmon's hymn'. This is the first recorded domestic English conversation.

The second text is a longer and more developed piece: *Ælfric's Colloquy* (his name pronounced [alf-rich]). A colloquy was a standard technique of instruction in European monastic schools, taking the form of a conversation between teacher and students. This one was written in Latin around the year 1000 AD by Abbot Ælfric of Eynsham, but someone later translated it into Old English, writing glosses for each word above the lines of the Latin text. The dialogue continues for 75 exchanges, at times capturing the rhythm of a quick exchange, with short questions and elliptical responses, as in this extract (my translation into Modern English):

TEACHER: What occupation do you have?
STUDENT: I am a fisherman.
TEACHER: What do you get out of your occupation?
STUDENT: Food and clothing and money.
TEACHER: How do you catch the fish?
STUDENT: I get on board my boat, and throw my net into the river and then I throw in my baited hook and wicker baskets, and whatever I catch I keep.
TEACHER: What if the fish are unclean?
STUDENT: I throw away the unclean ones and take the clean ones for my food.
TEACHER: Where do you sell your fish?
STUDENT: In the city.
TEACHER: Who buys them?
STUDENT: The citizens. I can't catch as many as I can sell.
TEACHER: What kind of fish do you catch?
STUDENT: I catch eels, pike, minnows and burbot, trout and lamprey, and whatever swims in water. Sprats.

> TEACHER: Why don't you fish in the sea?
> STUDENT: Sometimes I do, but rarely, because it takes a lot of rowing to get to the sea.
> TEACHER: What do you catch in the sea?
> STUDENT: Herring and salmon, porpoises and sturgeon, oysters and crabs, mussels, cockles, shellfish, plaice and flatfish and lobsters and many others like that.
> TEACHER: Would you like to catch a whale?
> STUDENT: Not me.
> TEACHER: Why not?
> STUDENT: Because it's a dangerous thing to catch a whale. It's safer for me to go to the river with my own boat than to go hunting whales with many ships.
> TEACHER: Why so?
> STUDENT: Because I would rather catch fish that I can kill than a fish that can sink and destroy with one blow—not just me but my friends as well.
> TEACHER: But many men catch whales and escape danger, and make a great profit out of it.
> STUDENT: You speak the truth, but I don't dare because of the cowardice in my heart.

Because of its length and varied subject matter, this colloquy has been called 'the first recorded English conversation'.

The impression we get, from looking back across the centuries, is that although individual words and expressions may have changed, the basic structure of a conversation hasn't really altered. 'Not me' (Old English *Nic*, a shortened form of *ne ic*) sounds so modern, for example. We can imagine that an Ethelred or Edwine would have had the same puzzled reaction as Steve in Chapter 1, if someone had given them a double 'good morning'—though in Anglo-Saxon times it would probably have been *good morn* (Old English *morgen*, similar to modern German), or later, *good morrow*. *Morning* isn't recorded in English until the thirteenth century.

Developing dialogues

Records of spoken dialogues really take off in the Middle English period, which is conventionally dated from the twelfth century until the mid-1400s. One of the most famous examples is an early thirteenth-century quarrel, in rhyming couplets, between an owl and a nightingale, as overheard by the poet. Here is a translation of their opening exchange, set as prose. The nightingale speaks first.

> 'Monster, you fly away. I feel sick when I see you. Indeed, because of your ugly face I very often have to stop singing. My heart fails and my tongue falters when you thrust yourself on me. I would rather spit than sing about your foul howling.'
>
> The owl waited until it was evening. She couldn't stay silent any longer, for her feelings were so powerful that she very nearly stopped breathing, and after a long time she spoke out.
>
> 'How does my song seem to you now? Do you think that I can't sing because I can't do twittering? You often make me angry, and say reproachful and shameful things to me. If I held you in my talons—and it could be that I might, if you were out of your tree—you'd sing a different tune.'
>
> The nightingale answered: 'If I stay out of the open, and protect myself against the hard weather, your threats don't bother me. If I keep myself in my hedge, I don't care at all what you say.'

And so the row continues, for a further 1700 lines, before they agree to have their arguments judged by a Master Nicholas of Guildford, who lives in Portesham in Dorset—presumably, the poet. The birds fly off to find him, but we never learn the outcome.

This was the first of many quarrels recorded in Middle English literature. The most ferocious were the harangues known as *flyting*, from an old verb *flight*, meaning 'to scold'. The word is still heard in northern English dialects and in Scotland, and it is in Scotland that the best literary examples survive, for in the late Middle Ages several Scottish poets engaged in formal exchanges of poetical invective, much enjoyed at court. A modern 'war of words' equivalent is the battle rap. But do contests of this kind deserve to be called conversations? The descriptions of the nature of conversation I quoted in my Prologue all suggest mutual cooperation rather than confrontation. This notion of a cooperative endeavour is perhaps unconsciously reinforced by the etymology of *con* 'with' (as in *connect, consensus, converge*...), so that, when the parties in an interaction are no longer maintaining some sort of shared intent, the word feels inappropriate. Certainly, everyday usage seems to support such an interpretation. The common expression 'the conversation turned into...' usually collocates with 'row, quarrel, argument, debate' and suchlike, as in this newspaper report (in the *Slovak Spectator*, May 2018) about a journalist's experience:

> While she thought it would be a friendly conversation to help their investigation into the murder, when she arrived at the police station, the conversation turned into a hostile interrogation.

I can't imagine anyone wanting to describe a debate or a quarrel as a 'conversation'.

Real conversations begin to appear in the prose narratives of the Middle English period. There are several in Thomas Malory's *Morte d'Arthur*, for instance. The conversational style is apparent from the very opening chapter (here shown in modern spelling and punctuation):

> Then for pure anger and for great love of fair Igraine the king Uther fell sick. So came to the king Uther Sir Ulfius, a noble knight, and asked the king why he was sick. 'I shall tell thee,' said the king, 'I am sick for anger and for love of fair Igraine, that I may not be whole.' 'Well, my lord,' said Sir Ulfius, 'I shall seek Merlin, and he shall do you remedy, that your heart shall be pleased.'
>
> So Ulfius departed, and by adventure he met Merlin in a beggar's array, and there Merlin asked Ulfius whom he sought. And he said he had little ado to tell him. 'Well,' said Merlin, 'I know whom thou seekest, for thou seekest Merlin; therefore seek no farther, for I am he; and if King Uther will well reward me, and be sworn

unto me to fulfil my desire, that shall be his honour and profit more than mine; for I shall cause him to have all his desire.' 'All this will I undertake,' said Ulfius, 'that there shall be nothing reasonable but thou shalt have thy desire.' 'Well,' said Merlin, 'he shall have his intent and desire. And therefore,' said Merlin, 'ride on your way, for I will not be long behind.'

Other early examples can be seen throughout Thomas Deloney's novel *Jack of Newbury* (1590s). In the opening chapter, John Winchcomb has a conversation with his master's widow. She's taken him into her confidence, and opens her mind to him about her suitors in a very natural-sounding conversation that moves along at a good pace:

> 'Although it becometh not me, your servant, to pry into your secrets, not to be busy about matters of your love, yet for so much as it hath pleased you to use conference with me in those causes, I pray you let me entreat you to know their names that be your suitors, and of what profession they be.'
>
> 'Marry John,' saith she, 'that you shall, and I pray thee take a cushion and sit down by me.' 'Dame,' quoth he, 'I thank you but there is no reason I should sit on a cushion till I have deserved it.' 'If thou hast not thou mightest have done,' said she, 'but faint soldiers never find favour.' John replied 'That makes me indeed to want favour, for I durst not try maidens because they seem coy, nor wives for fear of their husbands, nor widows doubting their disdainfulness.' 'Tush John,' quoth she, 'he that fears and doubts womankind cannot be counted mankind, and take this for a principle: all things are not as they seem. But let us leave this and proceed to our former matter. My first suitor dwells at Wallingford, by trade a tanner, a man of good wealth, and his name is Crafts; of comely personage and very good behaviour; a widower, well thought of amongst his neighbours. He hath proper land, a fair house and well furnished, and never a child in the world, and he loves me passing well.'
>
> 'Why then, dame,' quoth John, 'you were best to have him.' 'Is that your opinion?' quoth she. 'Now trust me, so it is not mine,

for I find two special reasons to the contrary. The one is that he being overworn in years makes me overloath to love him, and the other that I know one nearer hand.' 'Believe me dame,' quoth Jack, 'I perceive store is no sore, and proffered ware is worse by ten in the hundred than that which is sought. But I pray ye, who is your second suitor?'

And so the story begins, in a conversational style that could have come from any modern novel. The realism in these extracts comes partly from the colloquial tone introduced by interjections such as *marry* and *tush*, and such rhetorical expressions as *believe me, I pray ye, trust me,* and *why then*. And it's a short step from here to the full-scale dramatization of everyday conversation that we encounter in the same decade in the plays of Shakespeare and his contemporaries.

The quarrelling examples in this chapter raise the important point that came up in relation to greetings: what counts as a conversation? Evidently there are some types of dialogue that people would exclude from the notion, or, at best, consider marginal. Are there any others?

Battle rapping

The modern equivalent of flyting is the battle rap, in which contestants strive to outdo each other in exchanging improvised rhythmical and rhyming lyrics, typically insults and boasts in very strong language. In public competitions, winners are decided either by judges (*emcees*) or by audience acclamation. Here's a mild (and reasonably polite) illustration, which wouldn't win any competitions but does illustrate something of the various styles, with half-rhymes alongside full rhymes, and lines of different length:

> you think you good at rappin, but you better off at crappin
> you ain't got no chemistry, so you gonna feel jealousy
> take all the consequences, cos you got no defences
> you lookin at a writer, not a babyface reciter
> you gonna be in danger, battle rappin with this stranger
> who predicts your lousy tricks, cos he deals in linguistics
> you in a real fix
> you in the river styx
> doin things bove your station
> go take a vacation
> keep outta the heat
> I gonna spit on your feet
> turn you into mincemeat
> cos you're gonna be beat

Chapter Four

EXCHANGES

People who pass each other in the street, and who know each other, will routinely exchange a single-turn greeting—unless they have some personal reason for withholding it—typically a simple word (*Hello*) or comment (*Lovely day*), or even a non-verbal nod or wave. If they don't know each other, whether they'll say anything at all depends on the situation. If there are lots of people in the street, silence is the norm. We can hardly greet everyone, and anyone who tried to do so would be considered mentally unsound or promoting a special agenda, such as a beggar, religious enthusiast, salesman, or chugger ('charity mugger'). If the street is empty apart from the two passers-by, practice varies wildly. Some parts of a country are known for their readiness to greet; others expect silence. Several variables can alter local norms, such as an accompanying child or dog. Dog-walkers usually pass each other with some sort of verbal exchange, especially if their dogs engage in mutual sniffing.

Similar to streets are travel situations, such as queues, waiting-rooms, railway compartments, and adjacent seats in aeroplanes. Greeting exchanges, if they are made at all, are usually single-turn. So are family exchanges, as when someone makes a breakfast-time appearance or returns home from school or office, or after an evening out. There is a much stronger expectation of mutual oral recognition in domestic exchanges, of course. A failure to return a greeting signals that Something Is Up.

Greetings aren't the only kind of single-turn exchanges. Several situations present conventional routines that consist of just a request and an optional oral response. We buy a ticket from an unfamiliar clerk at a railway station. We tell a taxi driver the address we want to go to. We arrive at a gathering, and someone asks 'Can I take your coat?' There is no intention to continue the interaction, and in many settings it would be inappropriate to try to do so, especially if a queue is building up behind.

These exchanges would never be called conversations. To be a conversation, as I'll discuss later, there needs to be something more— a desire to inform or be informed, to develop a thought, to engage in some way. A topic has to be introduced other than the one used in the initial greeting, or it needs to be a significant development of it. And it has to continue for some time. When the interaction is limited to a single exchange, the distinction is clear enough. It becomes less clear when there is a short series of conventional exchanges, such as this one:

> I am sitting outside a pub in Stratford-upon-Avon, with a puppy on my knee. Someone leaving the pub sees the puppy and comes over, wanting to stroke it.
>
> PUB-LEAVER: May I? [strokes]
> ME: Sure.
> PUB-LEAVER: Lovely dog... How old is—he? she?
> ME: She. Three months.
> PUB-LEAVER: Gorgeous. What's her breed? Is she a spaniel?
> ME: No. A kooiker—a Dutch breed.
> PUB-LEAVER: Lovely. Thanks. [leaves]

Was this a conversation? There was a mutual expectation that the interaction would be short-lived. Neither party wished to develop the topic. It would surely be misleading if I were to say later, 'I had a conversation outside the pub today'. If I did, my listener might well ask, 'What about?' The answer would have to be 'About the puppy'.

But if the next question were 'What was said about the puppy?' I would be at a loss to answer, for there is nothing to report. 'It was just a chat', I might add.

Rituals

Routine exchanges would rarely be construed as conversations, even if they contained several turns. The word *first* is important in Dr Johnson's remark quoted in my Prologue: 'When two Englishmen meet, their first talk is of the weather.' This suggests that the opening content is not part of the conversation proper, and this is I think how most people would view it. But it is not only the weather that falls into this category of conversation openers. They also include person introductions, with their associated comments ('Pleased to meet you'), as well as exchanges in which a limited amount of personal information is provided, such as the affirmation of mutual contacts ('Mary's worked with Hannah', 'John and I sat on the same committee'), prior meeting checks ('Didn't I see you last year in Marienbad?'), and updates in family or friend reunions ('How's Doris these days?', 'How's Ben getting on?', 'You're looking well').

The word *ritual* is often used to describe these conversation openers, especially those intended to 'break the ice'. They are indeed, as the *OED* defines *ritual*, 'repeated actions or patterns of behaviour having significance within a particular social group', but the repetitions are definable only in a very general way, for there's a great deal of variation and unpredictability about the actual content and choice of expression of both the questions and the responses. In relation to content, in broadest terms the parties choose 'safe' topics—ones that are likely to elicit shared views, avoiding anything that might prompt strong personal opinions, generate emotional reactions, or provoke an argument. The subject matter has to be within the experience of both parties, so that both can make a contribution—which is why such topics as the weather loom large. In terms of expression, they will keep their sentences short, and their vocabulary conventional to the point of cliché ('Lovely day', 'Turned out fine again', 'Rain later')—features that help to explain the description of this kind of speech as 'small talk'. Intonation will be in their lower register; they will maintain a low loudness level and a measured speaking rate; and they will avoid tones of voice that convey marked emotions.

What counts as a 'safe' topic is not always obvious, however, and is dependent on the situation the participants find themselves in. Commuters on a train who read the same daily newspaper may consider the ease or difficulty of the crossword puzzle a safe topic. Commenting (positively) about decor is likely to be a safe topic for first-time visitors to someone's house. Complaining about the unreliability of trains is certainly a safe topic for most railway travellers. But any situation in which there is an element of 'shared suffering' will elicit exchanges about the experience that would not be encountered in other situations. A group of advertising executives attending a conference suddenly found a topic of mutual concern in front of a coffee machine that had ceased to behave itself.

It is the nature of ritual exchanges not to go on for very long, but the exact length is unpredictable, as it depends on personal background, personality, and (as in the case of the coffee machine) immediate circumstances. People who know each other are likely to keep the exchanges going for longer, as there will be an element of mutual recognition to deal with along with the choice of safe topic. People with different cultural backgrounds may have conflicting expectations about what makes a comfortable ritual exchange. In a working context, the need to get on with an agenda will truncate any opening ritual—and 'agenda' here is not restricted to the list of items to be covered in a formal business meeting, but to the mutual expectations that underlie any working situation, such as an interaction between a doctor and patient, or between a sales assistant and a customer. Personality enters in when one of the participants emerges as a joker, questioner, pessimist, complainer, activist, and suchlike. An innocent comment on the weather can segue into an unexpected diatribe about climate change, with the receiving party struggling to find a means of escape. This is when the notion of a 'one-sided' conversation arises (p. 52).

Rituals like these go well beyond the notion of *phatic communion* that has long been a recognized topic in linguistics. The term (from Greek *phatos*, meaning 'spoken') was introduced by anthropologist Bronisław Malinowski, who defined it as 'a type of speech in which ties of union are created by a mere exchange of words' (in an essay included in C. K. Ogden and I. A. Richards, *The Meaning of Meaning*, in 1923). The *OED* definition amplifies this, as utterances 'that serve to establish or maintain social relationships rather than to impart information, communicate ideas, etc.', adding that it is 'trivial or purely formal verbal contact'. Phatic communion thus has a very limited scope, identifying only those exchanges where the speakers are using language to establish rapport while disregarding the literal meaning of what is being said. Most of the above rituals, by contrast, do not disregard the meaning. On the contrary, meaning is essential in such cases as introductions.

The classic example of phatic communion is the three-part mutual health enquiry between people who do not have any reason to be concerned about each other's physical well-being:

MARY: How are you?
HELEN: Fine thanks, and you?
MARY: Very well.

Neither party is seriously interested in the other's health, and it would be distinctly odd if one of them were to launch into a detailed account:

MARY: Very well, though I do have a bit of a temperature today, and I'm still not entirely over the cold I had last week, and . . .

Old and new

There have always been several regional and slang alternatives to *how are you*, many in local pronunciations, such as (in the UK) *alright, how do, hey up, how you going, how you doing, how's it hang-ing,* and *whassup.* It was ever thus. In Shakespeare's day, we would encounter such greetings as *How, How now,* and *How do you,* as well as variants on modern *Good morning,* such as *Good dawning* and *Give you good morrow.* Not everything has changed: *Good day,* says Orlando to Rosalind (in *As You Like It*), Richard to King Henry (in *Henry IV Part 3*), and Benedick to Don Pedro (in *Much Ado About Nothing*), among many others. But we sense a social change when we observe other characters greeting each other with divine invocations, such as *God save you* and *God bless you,* something that is uncommon today. Archaic greetings are restricted to jocular greetings among friends (*Hail fellow, well met*). These examples illustrate that there have been changes in greeting ritual over the centuries; but it's unusual to encounter a change within a generation or two. That is why, when a new expression does come along, it attracts interest.

The latest example of this happening has been the addition of a new alternative to the range of expected responses to *How are you?*, allowing a contrast between *I'm well* (referring to one's physical state) and *I'm good* (referring to one's mental state). In fact the usage is older than people think, as the *OED* clearly shows. Take this dialogue:

GEORGE: I didn't see you, Aunt Ellen. How are you.
AUNT ELLEN: I'm good, thanks. You're looking well.

This is from Irish playwright Lennox Robinson's comedy *The Whiteheaded Boy* (1.23), published in 1921. The usage seems to have developed out of the much earlier expression *to feel good,* recorded in American writing from the early 1800s. In modern times it's been reinforced by a related use as a response to a question or request, meaning 'no, thank you' or 'I don't need anything':

BEN: Do you want another beer?
PETER: I'm good, thanks.

That's an American usage too, which seems to have developed in the mid-twentieth century (the *OED* first recorded usage is 1966). And probably because of its American origins, it evoked criticism from British language pedants. It was a curious reaction, because pedants are traditionally vocal when they perceive what they think to be a semantic distinction being lost (as when people use *uninterested* to mean *disinterested*). By contrast, *good* vs *well* is an example of a semantic distinction being gained, so pedants should have been pleased to see it rather than the opposite. But consistency has never been pedantry's strong point.

In all these cases, the mutual expectation is that the exchange will be short. The three-part health interaction can end there, with the parties saying nothing more to each other. Or, of course, they can move on to a conversation proper, which introduces a whole new set of expectations and strategies. But none of them would have thought of the comments made to each other about health, the weather, or the faulty coffee machine as constituting a conversation.

That paragon of conversationalists, Dr Johnson, would certainly deny that the exchanges illustrated in this chapter were conversations. James Boswell records in his *Life of Samuel Johnson* (III.449) an observation made in 1783:

> Though his usual phrase for conversation was TALK, yet he made a distinction; for when he once told me that he dined the day before at a friend's house, with 'a very pretty company;' and I asked him if there was good conversation, he answered, 'No, sir; we had TALK enough, but no CONVERSATION; there was nothing DISCUSSED.'

I imagine he was thinking of the kind of social chit-chat illustrated by Jonathan Swift (p. 10), which went on at some length. For Johnson, there has to be a great deal more than many conversational turns to count as a conversation. At around the same time, Boswell records a further reflection:

> Talking of conversation, he said, 'There must, in the first place, be knowledge, there must be materials; in the second place, there must be a command of words; in the third place, there must

be imagination, to place things in such views as they are not commonly seen in; and in the fourth place, there must be presence of mind, and a resolution that is not to be overcome by failures: this last is an essential requisite; for want of it many people do not excel in conversation.'

The criteria are useful, for they apply not only to interactions of the most intellectual kind but also to everyday chat. For two people to have a satisfying conversation about, say, tennis, they have to know what they are talking about, have some command of tennis vocabulary, have something fresh to say, and hold a point of view that they are able to maintain, even if they feel they haven't expressed themselves well. The criteria aren't complete. Johnson's view is very much that of a fluent speaker. He doesn't refer to the other critical element of a conversation: to be a good listener. William Hazlitt's remark in my Prologue comes to mind: 'The art of conversation is the art of hearing as well as of being heard.' But they do point the way towards a more sophisticated account of the nature of conversation.

An unusual exchange

Can you explain this sequence?

> **CHAIR:** John?
> **JOHN:** It's OK.

A business meeting is taking place. Twenty or so people are sitting around a long table. A paper has been presented and the discussion is taking place. Several of the participants have put their hands up and caught the eye of the chair, wanting to make a contribution. The chair has chosen who should speak in which order:

> **CHAIR:** Virginia, then Arthur, then John.

But by the time John gets his turn to speak, the observation he was wanting to make has been made by Virginia. He could, of course, repeat it, thereby reinforcing it. But he chooses not to, presumably thinking that the point has been made well enough, and it would only delay the meeting if it were reiterated. So his words tell the chair that he no longer wishes to speak, accompanying it with an acknowledging hand gesture and a negative shake of the head.

At a seminar sponsored by the European Union a few years ago, I learned a different method of communication. Everyone had a name plate lying horizontally in front of them. To show the chair that you wanted to speak, you placed this vertically on end. It's a sensible procedure when there are a lot of people around the table, and it becomes difficult to catch the eye of the chair. The weakness is that the chair can have difficulty monitoring the order in which people 'verticalize' their names, so that a name might be called long after a topic of conversation has moved on. A somewhat erratic thread can be the result.

> Topic X is being discussed, which has points A, B, and C.
>
> Eric wants to address point A.
>
> Chair doesn't notice Eric, and chooses Paula and James to speak, who focus on point B.
>
> Harry and Olivia signal they want to say something urgently about point B; the chair chooses them, and the discussion develops in that direction.
>
> The chair finally sees Eric, who addresses point A.
>
> The next speaker goes back to point B.
>
> Someone else then takes up Eric's comment on point A.

And so on. Sometimes several topics can become intermixed in this way. Chairs have a tough job keeping a meeting on track and coherent in such circumstances. Pity the person who has to write up the minutes.

Chapter Five

TAKING TURNS—OR NOT

Writing about conversation is difficult because one always seems to be stating the obvious, but the impression is deceptive. There are subtle rules and conventions at work in all conversations that we forget about because they are buried deep within our childhood past. We operate with them unconsciously, and only notice them when something goes wrong—a conversation becomes difficult or breaks down—and we struggle to explain the reason. Most people have had the experience of finding it difficult to start a conversation, or to end one; or have been put off from having a conversation because of the way their interlocutor has approached them. They often are unable to say why. When I ask people the question, 'What makes a successful conversation?', they find it an unexpectedly difficult question to answer because so many factors are involved. Each of Dr Johnson's four points hides a multiplicity of tiny linguistic issues, as well as some general strategies. They differ from language to language, and sometimes even within dialects of a language.

The most basic strategy is turn-taking, introduced at the end of Chapter 1. It seems like the most obvious thing in the world that we do not talk at the same time, and take turns to speak, but it is a behaviour we nonetheless had to learn. We did this early in the first year of life, and the way we did it has been demonstrated by video studies of parent–infant interaction made by such scholars as Colwyn Trevarthen at the University of Edinburgh. Basic routines, such as feeding and changing, introduce the baby to the turn-taking nature of language. This can be seen in the following extract from a recording I have of a 3-month-old at feeding time:

BABY [hungry]: crying

MOTHER [settling baby in arms and picking up bottle]: yes, yes, it's coming, it's coming, oh what a noise, what a noise... [gives baby the bottle]

BABY: drinks [mother silent, then after a while takes bottle away to pat the baby's back to get rid of any wind]

MOTHER [patting back]: there, that was good, wasn't it, now where's that little windy bobble? I think you've got a little windy bobble in there, haven't you...oh yes you have...

BABY: burps

MOTHER: there, good girl, that's a lot better isn't it [gives baby the bottle again]

BABY: drinks [mother silent]

It is primitive turn-taking. Baby makes noise—Mother speaks—Baby drinks (Mother silent)—Mother speaks—Baby burps—Mother speaks...and the pattern repeats. A similar turn-taking routine will be heard when the baby is being changed, and a little later the crying and burping will be replaced by cooing, babbling, giggling, and laughing. Simple interaction games (such as peep-bo) also involve a turn-taking sequence of stimulus and response. And eventually, at around age 1, the child's non-linguistic vocalizations become verbal, and something resembling a real conversation emerges, as in this exchange at 15 months (not showing immature pronunciations):

BABY [seeing her favourite bear]: teddy

MOTHER: there's teddy—on the chair [gives it to baby]

BABY [drops it]: down

MOTHER: oh dear, teddy's fallen down—silly teddy [picks it up]

BABY [delighted intonation]: teddy!

MOTHER: now you've got him—hold him tight—shall I give him a kiss?

BABY [holds teddy up to her face]: num num num

This has definitely got what Dr Johnson called 'materials', though not yet much of a 'command of words'. Some of the exchanges (such as the last one) are non-verbal. But the turn-taking is well established.

With language, rules always have to be ready to adapt to circumstances. So it makes an interesting exercise now to compare this basic turn-taking with real adult conversations. Sometimes, the behaviour is exactly the same, as can be seen in this extract from a published series of recordings made for the Survey of English Usage at University College London (see Preface). Two friends are discussing the forthcoming bonfire night (a forward slash marks the end of a major intonation/rhythm unit, a dot marks a short pause, and a dash a longer pause):

> MARY: I don't think we can m manage a a large – bonfire / but the fireworks / themselves / – er we have a little store of /
>
> JEAN: oh yes / they're quite fun / yes /
>
> MARY: mm / – yes the children like them / very much / so – I think as long as one is careful / – very careful / (JEAN: oh yes) it's all right /
>
> JEAN: mm /
>
> MARY: – but erm – I I I . I ban all bangers / . we don't have any bangers (JEAN: yes) / I can't stand those (JEAN: yes) / – just the pretty ones / –
>
> JEAN: sparklers are my favourites /
>
> MARY: mm / catherine wheels are my favourites / actually / but er – t you know we have anything that's pretty and sparkly /

It's a fairly slow-paced conversation, and the turn-taking is extremely regular. Even so, there are places where the two people talk at the same time. While Mary is talking about bangers, Jean is expressing her agreement with two *yes*'s (shown in brackets in the transcription). It's called *simultaneous feedback*, and it turns out to be an absolutely essential part of a successful adult conversation.

Quite a wide range of vocalizations is involved. While one person is talking, the other maintains a flow of feedback responses, especially if the speaker's turn is lengthy (as when telling a story). They are usually supportive in character (*mm, yeah, really, gosh, wow, oh no*...), and may be non-linguistic (laugh, whistle, audible intake of breath...) or non-vocal (head-shake, handclap, change in facial expression...). But if the conversation is going well, they will certainly be frequent. In the Survey recordings, there is one monologue about a driving accident (Recording 5), in which the listener gives the speaker 13 items of feedback during the 150 seconds of story-telling. In another, with different participants, a tale about a farm holiday (Recording 9) shows 22 vocal reactions in a slightly longer time-frame. This looks like one bit of feedback every ten seconds or so, but in fact the incidence of vocalizations varies greatly depending on the nature of what the speaker is saying. There may be none while the speaker is beginning a narrative, for instance, and many when the story reaches a dramatic climax. A lot depends on the fluency of the speaker: a hesitant delivery is more likely to elicit supportive noises. And of course, the number will grow if there is more than one listener. But some sort of simultaneous feedback is crucial.

It's possible for anyone to test this claim—though you have to be careful to choose people you know reasonably well, and who won't be disturbed by the experiment. Ask them to tell you a story of some kind, such as where they went on holiday, and react normally for the first few seconds, providing appropriate simultaneous feedback. Then withhold the feedback. Stop saying things like *mm* or *yeah*, maintain a straight face and avoid eye contact. They will immediately notice the change in your behaviour and feel uncomfortable. Whenever I've done this, the speaker has found it impossible to carry on with the story. They stop to check if all's well. 'Are you OK?', 'Sorry, am I boring you?', 'Have I said something wrong?' are some of the responses I've heard. To which the reply 'No, all's well, I was just testing a linguistic hypothesis' usually elicits an interested and sympathetic reaction—at least, I don't *think* I've lost any friends that way.

Successful conversations rely on simultaneous feedback. And this is one of the reasons we feel uncomfortable when we don't get any. If you've ever had an interview where the interviewer listens to you in stony silence, you will remember the discomfort—and the relief when what you're saying is given an affirming nod or *mhm*. It immediately boosts your confidence. Doctors learn (though seem to be rarely taught) that simultaneous feedback helps patients relax as they report their symptoms. And a lack of such feedback from youngsters can be a source of annoyance to adults attempting to carry on a conversation with them—though, having said that, we need to recognize that young children on the whole don't provide each other with simultaneous feedback or expect it from adults. I've read through dozens of transcripts made by child language acquisition researchers—a good example is Paul Fletcher's *A Child's Learning of English*, whose subject is followed from age 2 to 4—and there's no sign of it in the detailed transcriptions, nor in those of older children until they're into their teens. And even then, the instances are sporadic. Providing feedback seems to be a sign of mature social awareness.

Complementary speech

A rather different kind of simultaneous feedback is what I call *complementary speech*. Here's an example. In Recording 1 of the Survey, Tony is talking to Gerry about the quality of the stands in football grounds:

> but there was an interesting programme on these grounds / the way it showed talked about the continental ones / that one it / was it in Madrid / . they're superb / (GERRY: oh they're tremendous). and the way they could clear them in x number of seconds / . . . it was after that disaster you know / . (GERRY: Rangers /) I think he said there was only one modern ground in England / really / that could claim to be modern / was it Man City / – (GERRY: Coventry maybe /) or was theirs taken as one of the oldest / . . .

Gerry makes supportive and what he hopes are clarifying comments, shown in brackets, while Tony is speaking. (You have to imagine the overlaps—for instance, *Coventry maybe* is said at the same time as *or was theirs taken.*) Tony doesn't give them any acknowledgement, but continues in full flow. The difference from the *mhm* type of feedback is that he *might* have acknowledged Gerry's points—for instance taking up the Coventry reference a little later on. There is real knowledge (as Dr Johnson put it) here. But there is no turn-taking.

Nor is there any turn-taking in a further kind of overlapping speech. Two (or more) people say the same thing at the same time. Here's an example, from an episode of *The Prisoner* television series, 'The Girl Who Was Death'. In a lighthouse on a deserted shore, the Prisoner is captured by a mad scientist, Dr Schnipps, who dresses as Napoleon, and who plans to destroy London with a rocket, sending the Prisoner with it. This leads to the following exchange:

PRISONER: Oh the rocket, that reminds me, where is it?
SCHNIPPS: It is here.
PRISONER: Here?
SCHNIPPS: All around you...
PRISONER: All around us.
SCHNIPPS: The lighthouse itself...
PRISONER and SCHNIPPS: Is the rocket.

This is a typical 'light-dawning' situation: as a question is probed, one party anticipates the other, and both express the solution at the same time. When this happens, it's anyone's guess who will speak next.

Overlapping speech isn't always appreciated, especially when it becomes habitual. There are some listeners who have an uncanny ability to predict the last word or two of a speaker's sentence, while the speaker is saying it, and produce them at the same time, so that the effect resembles a chorus. Some people are equable when this happens to them, though in my experience most can't stand it—but are too polite to say so. On the plus side, it certainly shows that their listener has been paying close attention to what they've been saying. And paying attention is something that appears in another category of behaviour that interferes with the normal pattern of turn-taking: interruptions.

Telephone turns

Mark Twain sent out a Christmas greeting in 1890:

> It is my heart-warmed and world-embracing Christmas hope and aspiration that all of us, the high, the low, the rich, the poor, the admired, the despised, the loved, the hated, the civilized, the savage (every man and brother of us all throughout the whole earth), may eventually be gathered together in a heaven of everlasting rest and peace and bliss, except the inventor of the telephone.

When the telephone arrived, people were unsure how to deal with it, conversationally. Should one shout? Should one say 'Are you there?' or 'Guess who this is?' People were worried that they might receive calls from people to whom they had not been properly introduced. And etiquette books around the turn of the century were adamant that it was quite improper to send out social invitations over the telephone.

It took some time before the conventions of telephone conversation became established. The first phone directory (with 50 subscribers listed) was published in February 1878 by the District Telephone Company of New Haven, Connecticut, not far from where inventor Alexander Graham Bell worked. In November of that year, a 20-page directory included instructions for the correct use of the telephone that made several linguistic recommendations. The writers were clearly well aware of the importance of turn-taking:

- Should you wish to speak to another subscriber...commence the conversation by saying 'Hulloa!' When you are done talking, say 'That is all!', and the person spoken to should say 'O.K.'

- While talking, always speak slow and distinct, and let the telephone rest lightly against your upper lip, leaving the lower lip and the jaw free.

- When replying to a communication from another, do not speak too promptly... Much trouble ensues from both parties speaking at the same time...

- Any person using profane or otherwise improper language should be reported at this office immediately.

Chapter Six

INTERRUPTING

> Don't interrupt: it's rude.
> I wish you'd let me finish . . .

And at the end of one online etiquette site:

> Bottom line, don't interrupt others. It's rude, arrogant, and self-
> ish and usually doesn't win you many brownie points.

Interrupting, evidently, gets a very bad press. But these blanket generalizations miss a very important point: overlapping talk can be combative, but it can also be collaborative. If we consider Gerry's interventions in the Tony monologue on p. 40 as interruptions, then these are definitely cooperative: he is trying to help, and not to take over the conversation. The first linguistic studies of interruption largely took the view that all interrupting is a matter of competition—the metaphor of 'power' is regularly used, especially in discussions of gender differences. But when we examine recordings of the most frequently occurring kinds of conversation—in domestic settings—we find a very different state of affairs. Most of the interruptions are accepted as part of the normal give-and-take of social interaction. There is often an element of bonding—for example, a husband and wife might frequently interrupt each other, in telling a story, thereby showing listeners that they are 'one'. The following examples, all from the Survey of English Usage recordings, illustrate the range of attitudes that interruption can elicit. Apart from anything else, they show how frequent interruptions can be without causing harm to a conversation. On the contrary, they are signs of solidarity or rapport.

In the first transcription (from Recording 11), we see three interruptions in about twenty seconds of chat. The context is that Becky has read a newspaper report about new ways of organizing Christmas Day: the article suggested that it would be more convenient to have the main meal ('Christmas dinner') in the evening rather than at lunchtime. Her husband Chris has read about it too, and keeps chipping in—first with a clarification that Becky accepts, then with a fresh point that momentarily takes her aback. Their friend Anne intervenes to help Becky out, and is then in turn interrupted by Chris, but in a humorous way that sends the conversation in yet another direction. (In these transcriptions, the speakers are placed beneath each other, so that the points of intervention and overlap can be clearly seen.)

BECKY [referring to putting the turkey into the oven after a midday brunch]:
then you put your stuff on / . and you eat / – li in the evening –   six
CHRIS: about six or something /
        you know /
BECKY: o'clock or something / and you eat
CHRIS: in the middle of Billy Smart's
        Circus /
BECKY: well that's it / er well of course / I did think of that /
ANNE: but then I mean / isn't it a relief / to have an excuse for getting
        away from the television / cos one tends to have
CHRIS: and n n . no tea / – wait a minute / I'm just catch-
        ing up on this conversation / no Christmas tea /
ANNE [to Becky]: I can see you have problems

In the second transcription (Recording 8) we enter at a point where Amy has been describing, with some enthusiasm, how she was able to rid her house of mice, though her husband David hadn't approved of all her methods.

AMY: there was the mother unaccounted for /
        and one who'd escaped we'd seen go out/
DAVID: at least one / at least one/
AMY: one . I'm st . I'm being factual David /
DAVID: well it could have been – yes / well it could have been
        far more / – because there were
AMY: however / we thought it's in the garage/ ...

Amy shows her mild irritation by pronouncing *David* with a level tone, and presses on with her story. He tries to carry on with his point, but is put in his place with a firm *however*...and he doesn't interrupt again. But even here, the intention could not be seen as combative. David (not the author of this book, be it noted) is actually trying to help, and seems to have been rather disconcerted by his wife's dismissive response.

Examples like these give the lie to the negative view of interruption with which I began this chapter. The interrupters don't want to take over the floor. They are not denying the other person's right to speak. In an analysis of all the interruptions in the *Advanced Conversational English* recordings, I could see no instance where one speaker was being 'rude, arrogant, or selfish'. They were all cases of people developing ideas together, asking for clarification, sharing the answer to a question, and jointly contributing to a narrative. There were also a couple of instances where the aim of the interruption took on the character of a warning: Tony interrupts Gerry because he's noticed that Gerry's gestures might knock over a glass near the edge of the table, and he calls 'Watch out, Gerry...'. In another case, the reason for the interruption was to save the speaker time and energy, as the listener could see where the conversation was going: 'I get your point'—and the speaker realized he had no need to continue. None of this is to deny that violating interruptions exist, especially in situations where people are having angry rows or heated discussions, but simply to say that they are not the whole story—and indeed may only be a small part of the story. Our views to the contrary tend to be influenced by the constant quarrelling we see in television family soaps.

This alternative view of interruption is further supported by the way it may be accompanied by an apology or prompt one. An example of the first: a hostess realized that she needed to do something in the kitchen for their meal, and chipped in with: 'Sorry to interrupt, but I must just go and get something out of the oven.' An example of the second: a group is talking about taking the Eurostar to Paris:

JAMES: . . . and then when you arrive it's an easy trip by taxi to wherever as

ERIC [*interrupting*]: the trouble with taking a taxi is that you never know what the traffic's going to be like / especially getting from Paris Nord / – I always take the metro myself / [*makes eye contact with James*] sorry /

JAMES: yes / I was going to say / it's likely to be OK as long as the taxi queue isn't too great [*and continues*] /

'I was going to say' is one of the commonest ways of acknowledging the apology, and showing that a thread is being resumed after an interruption.

Clearly, the notion of interruption covers a spectrum of interventions ranging from the polite to the rude. The politest, I suppose, is a request for help, a need for clarification, perhaps, introduced by a self-effacing remark such as 'Sorry, I missed that'. Rather more aggressive would be a correction or confrontation, introduced by some such expression as 'Hang on', 'Whoa back', 'Wait a minute', or the like. But the force of the interruption will depend largely on the intonation with which it's said. A gentle, meditative 'Hang on', loudly but slowly said, with a low rising tone on the 'on', will convey empathy, a friendly challenge. A rapidly spoken version, with a hint of a shout, and a falling tone on the 'on', will be taken as confrontational or even aggressive.

Explaining interruptions is much more difficult than the early accounts suggest. It's not at all easy to interpret the reason for interruptions, and virtually impossible to generalize about them. Media accounts of interruption have focused almost exclusively on supposed gender differences. Men were supposed to interrupt women twice as often as the other way round, with this being interpreted as the expression of a masculine propensity for dominance and control versus a feminine propensity for empathy and connection. With many research studies now completed, there seems to be little support for a clear-cut gender contrast—a finding that won't surprise anyone who's been following the debate about male/female differences in conversation, beautifully summarized by Deborah Cameron in *The Myth of Mars and Venus* (2007). Too many other variables are involved. How well do the speakers know each other? Are there age or seniority differences between them, or cultural differences of some kind, or differences of personality? Has the speaker been monopolizing the conversation, thereby warranting an intervention, especially if the interrupter has a special claim to be heard (perhaps by being particularly knowledgeable about a topic)? Is there an underlying conflict situation, which will motivate interruptions? What are they talking about? Some topics are going to be more contentious than others. Where is the conversation being recorded, and do the speakers know they're being recorded? Many studies take place in a formal laboratory setting, which will be very different from the domestic situations illustrated above. In short, establishing the reason for an interruption requires an awareness of the entire context in which the conversation is taking place, and what has happened in that conversation before the interrupting moment.

The illustrations in this chapter have all been of cases where the interruption is made without the permission of the speaker. The listener simply breaks in. An alternative is to 'ask' for permission to interrupt, using body language to let the speaker know that someone else would like to take a turn. The commonest technique is to lean forward, with an audible intake of breath, perhaps the briefest of vocalizations (*erm, uh, I...*), and maybe with a hand movement to make the desire to speak even clearer. More than one cue may be needed if there are several listeners, and the potential interrupter has to attract the speaker's attention. It's then up to the speaker to accept or ignore the offer. Here too body language can play its part, along with tone of voice. Accept the interruption? A welcoming gesture, maintaining eye contact with the new speaker, and a slowing down of speech. Reject it? A negating hand gesture or head-shake, looking away, speaking more loudly and more rapidly.

The overlapping nature of most interruptions complicates any account of turn-taking. But it isn't the case that all interruptions overlap. Take this instance. Mike was telling what happened when his car had a breakdown on a motorway. He was clearly only halfway through his story when he paused to drink from his glass, and Arthur chipped in with an experience of his own. Mike waited patiently until Arthur had finished, and then carried on, launching into the second part of his story with the invaluable dismissive adverb, 'Anyway...'. This sort of intervention has to count as an interruption too, even though there's no overlapping.

Turn-banning

Turn-taking is such a natural phenomenon that it would seem inconceivable that anyone might be banned from participating in it. But there are situations where this happens, and one of the parties is, quite simply, not allowed to have a turn. The most obvious cases, I suppose, are those where the participants are not on an equal footing. British traditional court etiquette, for example, dictates that one does not talk to royalty until royalty has talked to one; and there are further constraints over the number of turns that are thereafter permitted. In such cases, which can be encountered in any strongly hierarchical section of society, the conversational ball (p. 5) remains with the senior participant, and is very firmly tied to a short piece of string.

The principle of 'not speaking until spoken to' in fact has a long history in relation to children. 'Children should be seen and not heard' is proverbial. An early reference is in a fifteenth-century book of homilies for feast-days (a *Festial*) by an English priest, Johannes Mikkus (John Mirk). In his text for the Feast of the Assumption, he refers to the Old English proverb 'A mayde schuld be seen, but not herd'. The context (the sermon is on a feast of Our Lady) suggests a view about the place of women, but *maid* was also sometimes used at the time for young virginal men, and it was not long before the proverb became generalized to children. While that particular injunction is no longer widely respected, other constraints on child turn-taking are still commonplace, such as 'don't speak with your mouth full' and 'don't talk to strangers'.

There are also situations where one of the parties chooses not to speak: in some legal systems, we have the 'right to silence', when being questioned, to avoid self-incrimination. In the USA this is referred to as the *Miranda warning*, after a 1966 Supreme Court judgment, and is widely known through innumerable dramatized crime stories— a typical expression being 'you have the right to remain silent, but anything you say will be taken down and used in court against you...'. The Fifth Amendment to the US Constitution protects individuals in this way ('nor shall any person...be compelled in any criminal case to be a witness against himself...'), and the principle entered everyday American speech in the mid-twentieth century through the idiom 'take or plead the fifth', said when someone wants to avoid answering an awkward question.

Conversation stoppers

One other scenario that interferes with the normal rhythm of turn-taking is when the listeners don't want to continue the sequence. Here's an example:

EMILY: It should be great. There'll be a band and all sorts.
PETER: We've got a spare ticket, so we were thinking...
EMILY: We're going to invite Jenny.
JOAN: She told me she was conceived in a car, you know.
Silence

Sometimes one of the participants in a conversation will make a totally unexpected remark, sometimes astonishing, often shocking or embarrassing, to which the others can make no rejoinder. It's called a *conversation stopper*: the natural flow of the conversation is interrupted. Usually, after a pause, if the topic isn't too serious, one of the participants will make a light-hearted remark acknowledging the impact in an attempt to get the conversation back on track. A change of topic is likely to follow. With a serious complication, such as if Joan had said 'She's got cancer, you know', it may completely derail the conversation and alter the mood, to the extent that the person who made the remark may be criticized by the others or feel it necessary to apologize.

The subject matter isn't always serious. The *Oxford English Dictionary* has a nice example, from actor Peter Bull's memoir *I know the face, but...* (1959):

> 'Do you do a lot of this kind of work?' I asked. 'Yeah,' he said. 'I was one of the apes in *Tarzan*.' This was a real conversation stopper.

A rather different kind of stoppage arises when one of the participants doesn't want to continue the conversation, as in a tense domestic or teetering romantic relationship. A single-word response to a complex question can be enough to end it, or the use of an expression of closure or postponement (*Sorry I asked, We'll talk about it tomorrow*), or, of course, giving no response at all. And it's difficult to imagine how a conversation can proceed comfortably if we've been presented with an unanswerable utterance:

> Are you looking at me?
> You used to be so slim.
> Tell me the truth. Am I stupid?
> Why isn't a pretty girl like you married?

It's a strategy that can be turned to dramatic advantage in literature (p. 71).

One-sided turns

There need to be two people at least to have a conversation? Not necessarily. What is happening in this recording?

> **HELEN:** oh yes / you're hungry / aren't you /
> *Silence*
> **HELEN:** I know / I know /
> *Silence*
> **HELEN:** I know / yes / it's dinner-time /
> *Silence*
> **HELEN:** and you know what this is / don't you / . . .

This is very like the mother–baby feeding-time conversation recorded on p. 37—its repetitive character and often exaggerated tone of voice are typical—but there's no child involved here. The listener is a dog and the emerging topic is a tin of dog food.

People routinely have conversations with their pets, and don't think it at all odd if the pet doesn't respond. Dogs are one of the exceptions, with tail-wagging and other behaviour showing some sort of awareness, and motivating further vocalization by the speaker. But in most pet situations—talking to a goldfish or a pet snake, for instance—there's no feedback at all, so that any interpretation of behaviour is totally within the imagination of the owner. And interruption is inconceivable.

Talking to a plant is a further remove, as in this example:

> you *are* thirsty, aren't you / I think Jeremy's not been looking after you very well while I was away / naughty Jeremy / [*pours water*] / there we are / that's a lot better / isn't it / [*pours a bit more*] not too much though / don't want you drowning / . . .

People do describe this sort of behaviour as a conversation, despite its one-sidedness. The topic is dictated by the situation. I suppose it's always possible for someone to have a conversation with their plants about the current political situation, as a form of self-help therapy. I can easily imagine a plant owner aggressively pruning a bush and saying crossly 'Well I bet *you* didn't vote for Brexit'—which raises the whole question dealt with in the next chapter: which topics are found in conversational situations?

The ultimate case of one-sided conversation must be talking to oneself. Oscar Wilde was a connoisseur: 'I often have long conversations all by myself, and I am so clever that sometimes I don't understand a single word of what I am saying.' At least, though, when talking to oneself, there is no interruption.

Chapter Seven

WHAT WE TALK ABOUT

For there to be a conversation, several factors have to be present. Obviously, there has to be a topic that is capable of continued treatment: Dr Johnson's 'materials', or his 'discussion' rather than just 'talk' (p. 32), or the cards that generate talk at conversation dinners (p. 17). Sometimes this emerges naturally out of the circumstances in which the participants find themselves. The coffee machine scenario described in Chapter 4 could lead to a conversation about machine failures in general. A comment about the weather could lead to a discussion of climate change. Circumstances will dictate the outcome—in particular, the time available. At work or in the street, we may well hear 'Terribly sorry, but I haven't got time for a chat' or other expressions of withdrawal. But time constraints aren't a factor in most everyday situations—at home, where members of a family are talking together or entertaining visitors, or away from home in a meeting place, such as a pub, restaurant, or community gathering.

In all such cases, there's one defining feature of conversation which places it apart from every other variety of language except literature (Chapter 13): its semantically random and unpredictable nature. We can, in principle, talk about anything we wish, and in no particular order. The topics encountered in a church, law court, business meeting, radio broadcast, and so on, and the sequences in which we encounter them, are largely dictated by the nature of the occasion, with only a limited amount of variation in subject matter expected or permissible. In some circumstances—giving evidence in court is a prime example—we can even get into trouble if we change the subject. The UK Home Office publishes a set of guidelines about giving evidence in court: its 2017 edition includes the recommendation 'avoid rambling, giving irrelevant information, and personal opinions'. Everyday conversation would hardly exist without copious use of all three!

We can talk about anything we wish? This would seem to be the default position for Lewis Carroll's Walrus (in *Through the Looking-Glass*), who is probably the most famous case in literature of someone affirming that a conversation contains a random collection of topics:

'The time has come,' the Walrus said,
'To talk of many things:
Of shoes – and ships – and sealing-wax –
Of cabbages – and kings –
And why the sea is boiling hot –
And whether pigs have wings.'

I suppose this could be construed as an agenda—we are going to talk about these topics and no others—for some conversations do begin that way: 'We need to have a talk about the holiday.' But I've always taken it to be an open-ended list, limited only by the constraints of the verse form—a case of no agenda, which is also quite common as a conversation opener: 'So what are we going to talk about?' The participants (in this story, the walrus and the naive oysters) simply have a mutual desire to talk to each other.

We can, *in principle*, talk about anything we wish. In practice, certain topics tend to be avoided—those that are likely to invoke deeply held beliefs or affiliations, or ones which could generate unease or embarrassment, such as problems at home, personal health, or career prospects. The traditional mantra is 'never talk about politics or religion'—with money, race, and sex sometimes added to the ban—and many people respect this. On the other hand, there are probably just as many who ignore it. G. K. Chesterton was one: in a 1927 newspaper article he told the story of George Bernard Shaw, who had been asked to take part in a discussion panel, whose rules forbad any discussion of politics and religion. Shaw replied that 'he never discussed anything else except politics and religion'. Chesterton commented, 'I also can claim that I never discuss anything except politics and religion', before adding, 'There is nothing else to discuss'. Ogden Nash was another, hinting at the distinction between conversation and gossip in his poem 'Never mind the overcoat, button up that lip' (1957):

> Persons who have something to say like to talk about the arts and politics and economics,
>
> And even the cultural aspects of the comics.
>
> Among persons who have nothing to say the conversational content worsens;
>
> They talk about other persons.

But circumstances can change attitudes, even among those for whom political topics are traditionally anathema. One of the most widely heard tropes in domestic conversations after the Brexit referendum vote in the UK was 'I never used to talk about politics, but now...'—and a lively discussion of the issue would follow (though usually short-lived, in the absence of expertise). In such situations, the political topic would often result in increased social bonding rather than discontent.

The anthology *Words on Words: Quotations about Language and Languages* has a whole section devoted to conversation. I've used some of the items in my Prologue, and here are some others that focus on the issue of 'what to talk about':

> If you are ever at a loss to support a flagging conversation, introduce the subject of eating. (Leigh Hunt, *Table-Talk*, 1851)
>
> For parlor use, the vague generality is a lifesaver. (George Ade, *The Wise Piker*, 1901)

A proverb is the horse of conversation; when the conversation droops, a proverb revives it. (*Yoruba traditional saying*)

The diverse semanticity of the genre, and its lack of constraint, is underlined by Max Beerbohm (in *Mainly on the Air*, 1946): 'Improvisation is the essence of good talk'—an observation that reminds me of Dr Johnson's third criterion (pp. 32–3): 'there must be imagination, to place things in such views as they are not commonly seen in'.

However, there's one set of circumstances where topic constraints are clearly present: in a formal setting, where the reason for the gathering is on everyone's mind, and where there's a recognition that the choice of topic has to be suitable to the situation. Under this heading would come interviews, consultations, seminars, and any form of counselling, as well as the conversations that follow a ritual, such as a wedding or a funeral. Here, notions of social decorum and appropriateness outrank other considerations.

Given all the variables that we've seen operating in the context of interruption (p. 48), such as personality and personal history, it would seem pointless to try to identify the specific topics that make or unmake a good conversation. I've always been a bit suspicious of the Chinese proverb 'There are 346 subjects for elegant conversation'. This is reminiscent of the 'chat packs' and 'conversation starters' that have proliferated online in recent years. One site offers 250 starter topics, such as:

What's your favourite way to waste time?
What would be your ideal pet?
If you could change your first name, what would it be?
What character in fiction would you like to be?

Useful as these can be when no topic naturally suggests itself, the most pertinent generalizations about conversation are those that focus on the content at a more general level: the bringing together of different knowledges and (something Dr Johnson does not mention in his four criteria, pp. 32–3) personal experiences. It is this sharing of personal background, the contribution of individuals, that lies behind all conversations that participants judge to have been enjoyable. That is why it's so important to give everyone an opportunity to contribute.

A certain suspicion hangs over the status of the individual contribution, due to the fear of 'the bore'. Ambrose Bierce, in *The Devil's Dictionary* (1911), must have had very bad luck with his conversations to come up with this definition of the genre:

> *Conversation, n.* A fair for the display of the minor mental commodities, each exhibitor being too intent upon the arrangement of his own wares to observe those of his neighbor.

Most people, indeed, have had the experience of being bored by a party in a conversation who talks too much and about only one subject. It's a frequent theme of essayists and pundits, and nobody has summed it up more succinctly than American musical comedy entertainer Lisa Kirk, in a 1954 magazine article:

> A gossip is one who talks to you about others; a bore is one who talks to you about himself; and a brilliant conversationalist is one who talks to you about yourself.

American statesman and man of letters John Hay, in his *Distich* number 13 (1871), made the same point linguistically:

> Who would succeed in the world would be wise in the use of his pronouns.
> Utter the You twenty times, where you once utter the I.

But the reality of life is that people do want to talk about themselves and their experiences, as well as hearing about the lives and experiences of others. William Makepeace Thackeray addresses the point directly, in *Framley Parsonage* (1860, Chapter 10). The narrator is reflecting on the way Lucy Robarts didn't fit into the usual mould of people. She was one of those few persons—for they are very few—who are contented to go on with their existence without making themselves the centre of any special outward circle. To the ordinary run of minds it is impossible not to do this. A man's own dinner is to himself so important that he can not bring himself to believe that it is a matter utterly indifferent to every one else. A lady's collection of baby-clothes in early years, and of house-linen and curtain-fringes in later life, is so very interesting to her own eyes, that she can not believe but what other people will rejoice to behold it.

The narrator (aka Thackeray) observes:

I would not, however, be held as regarding this tendency as evil. It leads to conversation of some sort among people, and perhaps to a kind of sympathy. Mrs. Jones will look at Mrs. White's linen-chest, hoping that Mrs. White may be induced to look at hers. One can only pour out of a jug that which is in it. For the most of us, if we do not talk of ourselves, or, at any rate, of the individual circles of which we are the centres, we can talk of nothing.

And he concludes:

I can not hold with those who wish to put down the insignificant chatter of the world. As for myself, I am always happy to look at Mrs. Jones's linen, and never omit an opportunity of giving her the details of my own dinners.

The balanced approach certainly worked for Thackeray, who was described by contemporaries as a brilliant conversationalist.

Changing the subject

As well as the randomness of the subject matter in everyday conversation, there is its inherent unpredictability: there is no way of knowing which way it's going to go. And at any point in the conversation we can switch topic to talk about something completely unrelated to what has gone before. It usually isn't done abruptly. There can be a brief warning, as in this next example. A group of friends have been talking about the rise in train fares, and one has been recounting a recent travel experience:

> KIM: ...it's ridiculous / the whole thing cost us more or less twice what we would have paid last year /
>
> RICHARD: that reminds me / I was in a shop in London last week / and found a copy of a book I'd been looking for for ages...

This book turns out to be about Richard's fishing hobby, and nothing to do with railway costs at all. Who knows what it was in Kim's story that made Richard think of this—but the point is that nobody in the conversation seemed to mind the topic shift. Nobody accused him of 'changing the subject'—that kind of comment tends to be made only when someone is trying to avoid an awkward topic.

That reminds me is one of the more open-ended markers of topic shift. *Speaking of...* will usually elicit a different but related theme. And there are several other ways of introducing a new topic of little or no relevance to what has gone before: *now you mention it..., by the way..., that sounds a bit like..., come to think of it...* These expressions are so unselfconsciously present that we don't realize their important role in helping to maintain a smooth conversational flow. One circumstance when we *do* notice them is when we've reached a fairly advanced stage in learning a foreign language, and realize that we lack a command of them.

There may be no warning of a topic change at all. An incidental occurrence during a conversation can cause a shift, without the need for any verbal alert, such as a sudden burst of rain or a clap of thunder. In a public space, surrounding events—the arrival of a meal in a restaurant, the siren of a passing fire engine, a goal in a football programme on a pub TV—can be enough to motivate a fresh topic. After the new event has passed, there may be an attempt to resuscitate the interrupted topic, and here too there are conventional expressions: *What were we talking about?, Another thing about..., Going back to what we were saying...*

A joke can be sprung on a group without any preparatory remark other than *Have you heard the one about...?* There's no requirement that the theme of the joke should bear any semantic relationship at all to what's just been talked about. A sudden thought can have the same outcome, as in this example (Recording 3) from *Advanced Conversational English*. Paul is sounding off about the way the press misrepresents foreign events:

> it annoys me no end reading newspapers / – really does / I get so irritated with almost everything / – if you start to read them – reasonably seriously / – er you start to see all the . the flaws / in what they're saying / and . if you've had an experience / or you've been on the spot / – and seen the difference / between the reality and what's reported / (ROB: mm) you can imagine what it is /
>
> ROB: yes / – well there you are you see / that's it
>
> PAUL: and how the whole thing blows up / rather like . have you you've read Scoop . have you /
>
> ROB: no /
>
> PAUL: Evelyn Waugh / because it's (ROB: no) – just like that / er it's very clever actually / it's one of . Evelyn Waugh's best I think / – because . . .

and he goes on to describe what the novel is all about. If you'd asked Paul and Rob, on their way in to this conversation, whether they would be talking about Evelyn Waugh that day, they would have been nonplussed, to say the least. Yet that's the sort of thing that happens in conversations all the time. The point is that the participants are prepared for this to happen, and accept the new direction for the conversation with equanimity—or even enthusiasm, if the conversation has been flagging.

One result of the randomness of an everyday conversation is that it can prove difficult to recall what was talked about after the event.

> ESTHER: had a nice chat to Joan in town today
> TOM: oh yes / – what did you talk about /
> ESTHER [*vaguely*]: oh – can't remember really / – this and that /

Esther is not being evasive. On that occasion there was evidently no particular reason to recall anything that was said. In an experimental situation, where the task is to *try* to remember, participants don't do very well. They may not even recall the topics when presented with a multiple-choice array. We might expect Rob, in the above example, to answer the following question correctly:

Which author came up when you talked to Paul this morning?
1 Harold Pinter
2 Evelyn Waugh
3 Martin Amis
4 Norman Mailer

Not necessarily. And in a different kind of experiment, carried out by psychologists researching into the nature of memory, we might ask Rob this question:

Which author came up when you talked to Paul this morning?
1 Harold Pinter
2 James Joyce
3 Martin Amis
4 Norman Mailer

The correct answer is 'none of them', but Rob—and many more—would nonetheless opt for one or other of them, or be easily persuaded. That is why it's important to be very cautious about how to treat conversational recall as evidence in a court of law. But this inability to recall what was said is actually a bonus, according to Dr Johnson, as Boswell records in his *Life*: 'The happiest conversation is that of which nothing is distinctly remembered but a general effect of pleasing impression.' And in another place, we read:

When I complained of having dined at a splendid table without hearing one sentence of conversation worthy of being remembered, he said, 'Sir, there seldom is any such conversation.' *Boswell:* 'Why then meet at table?' *Johnson:* 'Why, to eat and drink together, and to promote kindness; and, Sir, this is better done when there is no solid conversation; for when there is, people differ in opinion, and get into bad humour, or some of the company who are not capable of such conversation, are left out, and feel themselves uneasy. It was for this reason, Sir Robert Walpole said, he always talked bawdy at his table, because in that all could join.'

'What to talk about?' is one of the two major perspectives we need to explore when studying conversation. There isn't really a sensible answer to that question, given the 'several subjects of discourse, which would be infinite' (as Jonathan Swift put it, in an essay on conversation described below, p. 83). 'How to talk about it?' is the other. Here we can be much more specific, for behind all conversations there is a finite number of structures and strategies that participants employ with unselfconscious ease.

Topical allusions

Scene: Mike and Maria are looking at holiday brochures. Maria loves chocolate.

MIKE: That seems like a good offer.
MARIA: Mm.
[*Pause*]
MIKE: Like a chocolate?
MARIA: Thanks, but I don't feel like any just now.
[*Short pause*]
MIKE: Who are you, and what have you done with Maria?
[*Both laugh*]
MARIA: The hotel looks nice . . .

The implication is that the person has been taken over by some alien being that maintains human shape but alters personality. It's an unusual catchphrase, for its exact origin isn't known, though it must have originated in television or cinema science fiction. But since at least the 1980s it's been used in everyday conversation to express jocular astonishment when someone does something out of character.

If a catchphrase is dropped into a conversation, the speaker doesn't usually expect a response, other than a signal of recognition, such as a laugh. It is of course possible for Maria to try to explain herself, but she doesn't have to—and in this case she doesn't. The conversation can simply move on to a new topic, or continue with what was previously being talked about—in effect, ignoring the content of the remark and accepting it as a reminder of a shared experience.

The shared recognition is the important thing. Using a catchphrase is always tricky, because there's no guarantee that speaker and listener will be equally aware of the source, so there's always the risk of puzzlement, or worse, incomprehension, especially if the item is accompanied by an unusual tone of voice replicating the source, as in *Here's Johnny*. If you've not seen Jack Nicholson's character in *The Shining*, or are unfamiliar with its origin—the way Johnny Carson was introduced in *The Tonight Show* on US television—you would be at a loss what to make of it.

On the other hand, many catchphrases are transparent, in the sense that a listener unfamiliar with the source would still be able to deduce a relevant meaning. If you don't know the origin of *May the force be with you* (*Star Wars*), you should have no trouble working out that the utterance is a wish for your well-being, despite its curious phrasing. And likewise with *Make him an offer he can't refuse*, *Make my day!*, and *I love it when a good plan comes together* (from *The Godfather*, *Sudden Impact*, and *The A Team*, respectively). Breakdowns in communication are more likely to occur if an unknown name is involved. The following exchange actually happened:

Scene: Father helping with his 15-year-old son's homework

SON: But I still don't get it.
FATHER: Elementary, my dear Watson.
SON: Why are you calling me Watson?

It's actually quite difficult providing an explanation to someone who has never heard of the stories by Arthur Conan Doyle and has little or no idea who Sherlock Holmes was—though that scenario has become easier since the success of the television series starring Benedict Cumberbatch. Other names might pose less of a problem. Could the following ever happen?

Scene: A washing-machine has made an unusual noise and stops

MARY: Hilary, could you come and take a look at this?
Hilary comes over, opens it up, and looks inside
HILARY: Houston, I think we have a problem.
MARY: Why are you calling me Houston?

And if a risqué allusion isn't recognized, the conversation might well break down into an embarrassed silence:

> *Scene: Sarah, at a reception where a waiter is offering canapés, squeals with delight after eating one.*
>
> **SARAH:** Mm.
> **CLAIRE:** I'll have what she's having!
> *All laugh*
> **SARAH** [*puzzled*]: What's so funny?

She clearly hasn't encountered the restaurant scene in *When Harry Met Sally*.

Chapter Eight

HOW WE TALK ABOUT IT

Normal domestic conversation isn't like the balanced, equable dialogues so often seen in textbooks that teach English as a foreign language:

> A: I haven't seen you for ages.
> B: I've been travelling a great deal.
> A: Where have you been?
> B: We spent three months travelling around Australia.
> A: Wonderful. I've never been there.
> B: You really should go.
> A: It's a fantastic country, so I've read.
> B: It is indeed.

Conversations of this kind have a recognized pedagogical value, but students shouldn't be given the impression that real conversations among adults at home are anything like that.

Nor are they like the succinct give-and-take of many a play script:

> LORD CAVERSHAM: Why don't you try to do something useful in life?
> LORD GORING: I am far too young.
> LORD CAVERSHAM: I hate this affectation of youth, sir. It is a great deal too prevalent nowadays.
> LORD GORING: Youth isn't an affectation. Youth is an art.
> LORD CAVERSHAM: Why don't you propose to that pretty Miss Chiltern?

LORD GORING: I am of a very nervous disposition, especially in the morning.

LORD CAVERSHAM: I don't suppose there is the smallest chance of her accepting you.

LORD GORING: I don't know how the betting stands today.

LORD CAVERSHAM: If she did accept you she would be the prettiest fool in England.

LORD GORING: That is just what I should like to marry. A thoroughly sensible wife would reduce me to a condition of absolute idiocy in less than six months.

LORD CAVERSHAM: You don't deserve her, sir.

LORD GORING: My dear father, if we men married the women we deserved, we should have a very bad time of it.

This extract from *An Ideal Husband* bounces along wonderfully on stage, but it would be rare to hear such witty repartee around the dinner table—or, if it did occur, it would take up only a small part of the whole conversation. Oscar Wilde's dialogue is a beautifully crafted piece of art, but it's not everyday conversation as most of us know it.

What makes these extracts so different? Their length and their balance. Measured in words, the first extract is 6 – 6 – 4 – 7 – 5 – 4 – 7 – 3. The second is 10 – 5 – 15 – 8 – 9 – 11 – 12 – 8 – 13 – 27 – 5 – 20. The conversational turns are quite short, and there is little difference between the amount each participant speaks: A's total wordage is 22, B's 20; Lord Caversham's is 64, Lord Goring's 79. And these totals are characteristic of much dramatic writing—unless someone is explaining something, for the sake of a plot, or giving a speech to show character, when the turn is likely to be longer.

The contrast with the kind of domestic conversations recorded for *Advanced Conversational English* is striking. Take the football conversation I illustrated on p. 40 (presented in its full form in the Appendix, p. 193). Together Gerry and Tony speak 1044 words in just over six minutes. Their roles seem to be fairly well balanced: G speaks 483 words, T 561. Each would presumably say, if asked, that they had been able to make a good contribution to the conversation.

But it is the array of lengths that needs to be noted. There are 17 turns in the extract, which would—if the balance of the ELT dialogue was being followed—be 61 words per turn. In fact what we get is this:

```
T    G    T    G    T    G    T    G    T    G    T    G    T    G    T    G    T
35 - 281 - 7 - 26 - 14 - 53 - 371 - 22 - 34 - 50 - 7 - 10 - 52 - 19 - 9 - 22 - 32
```

It is an erratic, patternless sequence, at any one point displaying no balance at all. There are two lengthy speeches—one of them taking over two minutes—but this is a natural consequence of someone expounding a point of view. When telling a story, imbalance becomes even greater. For example, the conversation extract about mice (p. 46) also lasts about six minutes, and Amy speaks for five of them—but then, it *is* her story. And the point is: nobody minds. It's clear from the reactions—the mutual affirmations of points being made, the occasional laugh—that all are enjoying themselves. Which is why they are having the conversation in the first place.

Being fuzzy

There is a second big difference between the kind of dialogue we see in typical ELT and play dialogues and that which occurs in domestic conversation: the participants' lack of interest in precision—or, putting this another way, their penchant for semantic fuzziness. Ambiguity, inexplicitness, vagueness, approximation, leaps of thought, gaps in explanation, even self-contradiction are all perfectly normal. The conversations I've been using as illustrations so far are full of expressions such as the following:

- o it sounds a bit like where we're living in a way / – not like that entirely /
- o you remember what Sheana said about the trees and the etcetera /
- o Susie said – that there were no such things as fairies / elves / this that and the other /

- nice savory things / you know / – bits of nice bacon / <u>and all that</u> /
- you eat in the evening / six o'clock <u>or something</u> /
- there's been a great hooha about it / recently / about a film that was made / <u>and so on</u> /
- a rather boring game of football / with no personality/ and all defensive / <u>and everything</u> /
- you're not going to <u>sort of</u> knock it all down / and build it from scratch /

They are especially common at the end of a sentence. The speakers have given an example of the main point they're making, and evidently don't feel the need—or haven't got the mental energy—to provide other examples that would be relevant. There may even be an admission of total semantic surrender:

somewhere in America / – I've forgotten the details now /

The important thing to note is that the lack of clarity doesn't result in an increase in the number of requests for clarification. There seems to be an unconsciously held acceptance that approximation is normal, and further detail is unnecessary. So we never find such sequences as:

BECKY: you eat in the evening / six o'clock <u>or something</u> /
CHRIS: sorry Becky, but does 'or something' mean 5.45 as well as 6.15 / or are you just thinking of 6.05 or 6.10 /

We might think that if conversations are going to be full of fuzziness, then they will also be full of questions to get rid of the fuzziness. This is a myth reinforced by such texts as the English-teaching dialogues, where questions are an important device to give students conversation practice, and plays, where questions are a useful way of giving audiences plot information. ELT dialogues fuel the impression that questions are common, as they focus on exchanges where information is needed, such as asking the way, enquiring about the price of goods in a shop, or finding out about the history of London.

And quick-fire question-and-answer exchanges are a major element in a play like Harold Pinter's *The Birthday Party*:

GOLDBERG: Webber, what were you doing yesterday?
STANLEY: Yesterday?
GOLDBERG: And the day before. What did you do the day before that?
STANLEY: What do you mean?
GOLDBERG: Why are you wasting everybody's time, Webber? Why are you getting in everybody's way?
STANLEY: Me? What are you –
GOLDBERG: I'm telling you, Webber. You're a washout. Why are you getting on everybody's wick? Why are you driving that old lady off her conk?

And so it continues, with questions constituting over half of the next hundred turns.

Many take the form of 'unanswerable questions'—a technique Pinter uses in this scene to reduce the verbal and cheeky Stanley to a state of inarticulateness.

GOLDBERG: Is the number 846 possible or necessary?
STANLEY: Neither.
GOLDBERG: Wrong! Is the number 846 possible or necessary?
STANLEY: Both.
GOLDBERG: Wrong! It's necessary but not possible.
STANLEY: Both.
GOLDBERG: Wrong! Why do you think the number 846 is necessarily possible?
STANLEY: Must be.
GOLDBERG: Wrong...

An unanswerable question is always a sign of a potentially dangerous situation. Compare the following two scenarios. You are approached by a stranger in the street:

STRANGER: excuse me...
YOU: yes?
STRANGER: can you tell me the way to the bus station?

You try to help.

> STRANGER: excuse me...
> YOU: yes?
> STRANGER: is it raining in Melbourne?

Now you look around nervously for help. Any unanswerable question is a threat, and Pinter, as the apostle of dramatic menace, uses the device to great effect in his plays.

This is all brilliant drama, but in no way indicative of what goes on in normal conversation. In domestic settings, questions turn out to be surprisingly rare. They will regularly initiate a topic, but will hardly be used after that—otherwise the conversation would turn into something resembling a Goldberg interrogation. For example, here are the questions that begin two of the conversational extracts from *Advanced Conversational English*:

Andy asks: what's the failure with the football /

Gerry provides 30 lines of response, ending with a comment about deterioration in the grounds.

Tony then asks: in what way have conditions deteriorated Gerry /

and this leads to 90 more lines of shared chat, with no further questions.

At the beginning of the newspaper conversation quoted earlier (p. 61), Paul tells Rob about hooliganism in the UK and asks him:

did you get that in Cyprus / did you hear about it /

There are then over 100 lines of chat before another question (about *Scoop*) initiates a topic shift.

All the conversations in the book are like this. A single question (or a statement which has the force of a question) generates a large amount of response, with the other party/parties in the conversation evidently feeling that further questions are unnecessary to keep it going. It's very unusual for a conversation to be punctuated with a series of questions asking for clarification. And even the opening

can be question-free, with a topic introduced by a general statement
of some kind.

> spectator sports are dying out / I think /
> we're looking forward to Bonfire Night /

Question-sequences are of course going to occur at the beginning of
a conversation where the parties don't know each other, or haven't
met for some time, or where there is a real need for information
(such as how to travel from A to B); but in everyday domestic chat,
they are conspicuous by their absence. As Dr Johnson put it to
Boswell, 'Questioning is not the mode of conversation among
gentlemen'.

Being parenthetic

By contrast, domestic conversation is full of what grammarians
sometimes call *comment clauses*—the kind of expression illustrated by
you know, *you see*, and *I mean*. These are always parenthetic, and their
job is to give listeners some clues about how the speaker is thinking.
In the six minutes of the Gerry/Tony conversation, there are 29
instances: 19 *you know*, 9 *I mean*, and 1 *you see*. And there is a double
use of *you know* and *I mean*. Gerry has just described the narrow
width of an exit gate at a football ground, and finds himself lost for
words to describe the danger:

> about thirty thousand have to go out through there / you know /
> I mean er – oh it's terrible /

The *you know I mean* or *I mean you know* sequences are very common
in everyday conversation when people are groping for the best
words to say what they have in mind. In such a setting, they would
never be noticed. They act as a kind of linguistic oil to make the
conversation flow smoothly, pointing in both directions, to speaker
(*I mean*) and to listener (*you know*), and bringing them together into
a close relation. They are, in effect, an affirmation of mutual trust: by

using *I mean* Gerry is asking Tony to accept his difficulty in finding the right words; by using *you know* he is telling Tony that he doesn't need to find any more words because Tony is intelligent enough to work them out for himself. Comment clauses only ever get noticed when overused, or used in public domains such as radio interviews, where we expect people to be able to express their thoughts clearly. Then they can and do attract listener criticism.

There are dozens of comment clauses in English, expressing a wide range of meanings, and appearing in first, second, and third persons. They vary somewhat in formality, from the highly colloquial *I'm afraid* to the self-consciously formal *one hears*, and in rhetorical force, from the mildness of *I dare say* to the earnestness of *it grieves me to say*. I can't imagine a conversation without several of the following:

- tentativeness, with reference to oneself: *I suppose, I think, I believe, I suspect, I guess, I dare say, I wonder, I ask myself, as I understand it*

- tentativeness, with reference to others: *they tell me, it's said, it's rumoured, as it seems, as I see it, one hears, as they say, as I'm told, it's alleged, it's been claimed, loosely speaking, speaking generally*

- certainty: *I know, I must say, I'm sure, I remember, I've no doubt, I have to say, you can be sure, as you know, it's true to say, it transpires, there's no doubt*

- emphasis: *as I say, as I've said, as I pointed out earlier, putting this another way, putting it bluntly, stated quite simply*

- emotional attitude: *I hope, I fear, I'm afraid, I'm glad to say, I'm happy to tell you, it grieves me to say, what annoys me, what's very surprising, to be honest, to be serious for a moment, frankly speaking*

- drawing attention, in a friendly way: *you know, you see, mind you, you realize, you may have heard, it may interest you to know, as it happens*

- asking for agreement: *you must admit, wouldn't you say?, don't you agree?, as everyone knows, as you say, if you like.*

Some comment clauses are quite famous, and get into any book of quotations, such as Henry Morton Stanley's greeting, when he tracked down David Livingstone in Africa: 'Dr Livingstone, I presume?' Others are important character notes in literature. Launce in Shakespeare's *Two Gentlemen of Verona* (4.4.10), for instance, is a great comment clause user, as seen in his monologue where he is complaining about the behaviour of his dog, Crab:

> I would have, <u>as one should say</u>, one that takes upon him to be a dog indeed, to be, <u>as it were</u>, a dog at all things. If I had not had more wit than he, to take a fault upon me that he did, I think verily he had been hanged for't; <u>sure as I live</u>, he had suffered for't. You shall judge. He thrusts me himself into the company of three or four gentlemanlike dogs under the Duke's table; he had not been there, <u>bless the mark</u>, a pissing while but all the chamber smelt him.

Examples like this show how some of the expressions have been in the language a very long time.

In any conversation, *you*-forms are likely to be used twice as much as *I*-forms (as in the Tony/Gerry extract). Much less common are the third person ones, beginning with *it*, *one*, or *they*, and those beginning with *as* or *to*—though individual speakers often have a preference for one or other of them. I know a local councillor who can't resist inserting a *to be honest* into his speech every few seconds. But they all combine to make comment clauses one of the most important features of conversation. Most are highly colloquial in character; but some—those of the type *to be frank* and *frankly speaking*—tend to occur in rather more formal conversations, or in writing. Academic writers often use them to soften the force of their generalizations, or to deflect a potential criticism of overstatement. I do it myself. There's an example in the next sentence.

Dramatists, it would seem, avoid a wide range of comment clauses in their plays. We can read pages of dialogue without encountering any. In Harold Pinter's *The Birthday Party*, there's just one instance of *you know* in the entire play, compared with the 19 *you know*s used by Gerry and Tony in six minutes, and only four instances of *I mean* compared with their nine. I choose Pinter as my example because he has been praised more than most for his 'tape-recorder ear'. But the kind of sentences his characters speak, hugely effective as they are in creating atmosphere, don't achieve their powerful effect through the use of comment clauses.

Comment clauses aren't the only kind of conversational fuzziness, of course. Also frequent are words and phrases that express approximation or introduce a degree of indefiniteness, such as *for the most part, hardly ever, seldom, often, sometimes, somewhat, in some respects, to some extent, a bit, more or less, in a sense.* These are also sprinkled liberally throughout domestic chat. And their function, along with that of the other features in this chapter, is essentially to make things easier, for both speaker and listener. The seventeenth-century statesman and essayist Sir William Temple, in his 'Heads designed for an essay on conversation', links ease and enjoyment:

> In Conversation, Humour is more than Wit, Easiness more than Knowledge; few desire to learn, or think they need it; all desire to be pleased, or, if not, to be easy.

Fuzziness is one way of achieving this aim. How else is this ease achieved?

Enjoy!

Great writers down the centuries affirm that the primary function of conversation is enjoyment.

> The more the pleasures of the body fade away, the greater to me is the pleasure and charm of conversation.
>
> (Plato, *The Republic*, 4th c. BC)

> It is a peculiarly satisfactory experience for a man to take pleasure in conversation and seek to excel at it.
>
> (Cicero, *On the Orator*, 1st c. BC)

> To my taste the most fruitful and most natural exercise of our minds is conversation. I find the practice of it the most delightful activity in our lives.
>
> (Michel de Montaigne, *On the Art of Conversation*, 1570s)

> Conversation...so useful and innocent a pleasure, so fitted for every period and condition of life, and so much in all men's power.
>
> (Jonathan Swift, *Hints towards an Essay on Conversation*, c.1713)

> There is in this world no real delight (excepting those of sensuality), but exchange of ideas in conversation.
>
> (Samuel Johnson, in Hester Lynch Piozzi, *The Anecdotes of the late Samuel Johnson*, 1786)

> The best of life is conversation, and the greatest success is confidence, or perfect understanding between sincere people.
>
> (Ralph Waldo Emerson, *The Conduct of Life*, 1860)

There can be no fairer ambition than to excel in talk; to be affable, gay, ready, clear, and welcome.

(Robert Louis Stevenson, *Talk and Talkers*, 1882)

Theodore Zeldin, in *Conversation* (1998), has a more ambitious set of aims:

Conversation has to explore new territory to become an adventure....

Conversation changes the way you see the world....

You start with a willingness to emerge a slightly different person.

Chapter Nine

TAKING IT EASY

The length of a conversation is unpredictable. The ones from which I took the extracts in *Advanced Conversational English* varied enormously, from half an hour to over two hours—the latter punctuated by events such as the arrival of coffee or the antics of a dog. But whatever the length, if the flow of a conversation is to be maintained, the participants need to make things easy for each other. My quotation from William Temple, at the end of the last chapter, could be supplemented by the observations of many others about what drives a successful conversation. For instance, there's the neat analogy made by American actress and writer Margery Wilson in *The Woman you Want to Be* (1928):

> Conversation is much like a tennis game except that in tennis you try to put the ball in the most difficult position for the one who must hit it while in conversation you must try to put it where it will be easy to hit.

Ease is a recurrent theme.

The default assumptions behind such remarks are that each participant in a conversation wants to be there, and wants to cooperate in making the conversation work as smoothly as possible. There are of course occasions when one or other of the group is an unwilling presence, or wants to be awkward, but I take these to be special cases. Conversations that become uncomfortable do need to be analysed to see if we can work out what has gone wrong. But most conversations don't start out that way. When people enter into a conversation, the normal hope and expectation is that they are going to be nice to each other, and that all will be well. 'The soul of conversation is sympathy', said William Hazlitt in *The Plain Speaker* (1826). Today we would say 'building rapport'.

Conversations, like stories, have a beginning, a middle, and an end, and any notion of 'ease' has to apply to all three. The beginning poses least difficulty. Any problem we encounter when engaging in a conversation is not how to start it but how to keep it going and how to end it. Writers often say the same thing about their plots. A review of a novel may spot weaknesses, and make such remarks as 'starts well enough...flags in the middle...didn't know how to end it'. Post-mortems on conversations can generate similar concerns about the middle and end: 'We were getting on well until...' or 'Never thought we would get away'.

Beginnings

The starting-point is typically unproblematic because it is a natural outcome of the situation in which people find themselves when they arrive at a house, a dinner table, or wherever. There will be a phase of greeting, some initial phatic communion (p. 30), and probably some genuine enquiries about health, children, friends, travel, the surrounding decor, and the like, depending on the relationship between the participants and the circumstances in which the conversation is taking place. If the participants meet often (as in family settings), the shared background will make opening remarks minimal or non-existent. If they don't know each other, the need to establish some common ground will be a priority, along with an awareness of 'who they're talking to'.

This is more than just politeness. Mutual awareness brings to light which topics might fruitfully be initiated—and also which should be avoided. Learning that the person sitting next to us at a dinner table is a surgeon will prompt us, if we have only an amateurish knowledge of medicine, not to make naive or inappropriate remarks about medical issues, and give us an instinct to defer to others, were the conversation to move in a medical direction. Oliver Wendell Holmes' remark in my Prologue applies: 'The whole force of conversation depends on how much you can take for granted.'

The aim is to establish rapport as quickly as possible. That is the fundamental role of phatic communion, as we saw in Chapter 4. Dr Johnson's comment about the weather, also quoted in my Prologue, is expanded in this way:

> It is commonly observed, that when two Englishmen meet, their first talk is of the weather; they are in haste to tell each other, what each must already know, that it is hot or cold, bright or cloudy, windy or calm.

Such exchanges clearly should not be judged in informational terms for no new content is being exchanged. Rather, it demonstrates the willingness of the speakers to collaborate, and thus lays the ground for the first topic of the conversation, whatever it will be—something that participants in rapport will each be able to contribute to.

Finding common ground is usually a natural and unselfconscious process, arising out of the sharing of past experiences. That's why I quoted from Sarah Orne Jewitt in my Prologue:

> Conversation's got to have some root in the past, or else you've got to explain every remark you make, an' it wears a person out.

This is what makes conversational topics different from phatic communion, which is always grounded in the present—a remark about the weather, health, travelling conditions ('Busy train again today'), the state of a game ('Playing well, aren't they'), and so on. As Dr Johnson says, it's talk about what everyone knows about. A valued conversational topic, by contrast, has to be about something everyone doesn't know about, or perhaps can't remember—or, at least, one that allows each participant to say something they believe the others would want to know, derived from their past experience.

This often takes the form of an illustration or explanation of what has just been said, based on the speaker's recall. It's not always new knowledge that's being shared. Often it's something which other participants are well aware of, but which they have forgotten or left unstated. We can see this happening in the following extract (Recording 7) where a group of friends are talking about how (in the 1970s) it was possible to take a car across the English Channel. Mark (who's never done it) has said he's heard it's 'hell', and John (who often has, along with Beth) has responded by describing how it's never been a problem for them. The references to their personal pasts are underlined. (Simultaneous feedback vocalizations are omitted in this transcription.)

> MARK [*illustrates*]: well I'll tell you the sort of thing I've heard / I mean ev every summer / . er you you see stories of tremendous queues at the
>
> JOHN [*explains*]: but they're people who haven't booked / –
>
> BETH [*affirms*]: yeah /
>
> JOHN [*illustrates*]: mind you / last summer / there was a weekend when / . i . th the queues were so bad / that even people who'd booked / couldn't get to the boats /
>
> PETER [*explains*]: and yeah it was something to do with the strike though / wasn't it /
>
> JOHN [*affirms*]: yeah . there was / there was there was some . some trouble / as well / yes / that's right /
>
> BETH [*restates John's original account*]: but certainly / in the past / we've just rolled up /...

Several things are going on at the same time. John has hitherto been very positive that there isn't a problem, but is ready to acknowledge that there is some justice in Mark's objection. His illustration of queuing is, in effect, a point against himself. And his next remark shows that he knows there had been a strike, but it takes Peter to remind him. It's a short exchange, but it shows two important features of a successful conversation: its collaborative nature (Peter helping John out) and its face-saving character (John acknowledging that Mark may have a point). They are features that will appear from the very start of any successful conversation, and permeate it. They are also the features that will be most disregarded, if—for whatever reason—the conversation doesn't go according to plan.

Middles: going wrong

Jonathan Swift devoted an entire essay to the things that can go wrong during a conversation. Written in 1713 or thereabouts, he called it 'Hints towards an essay on conversation'—a nod to the title used by Sir William Temple (p. 76), whose private secretary he was. He begins by castigating those who monopolize:

> Nothing is more generally exploded than the folly of talking too much; yet I rarely remember to have seen five people together, where some one among them has not been predominant in that kind, to the great constraint and disgust of all the rest.

He makes the point, often forgotten about in discussions about conversation, that monopolizing isn't restricted to one person. Two people can just as readily monopolize:

> I often have observed two persons discover, by some accident, that they were bred together at the same school or university; after which the rest are condemned to silence, and to listen while these two are refreshing each other's memory, with the arch tricks and passages of themselves and their comrades.

He goes on to describe the focus on *I* rather than *you*, which I discussed when the subject of bores came up in Chapter 7.

> Another general fault in conversation, is that of those who affect to talk of themselves: Some, without any ceremony, will run over the history of their lives; will relate the annals of their diseases, with the several symptoms and circumstances of them; will enumerate the hardships and injustice they have suffered in court, in parliament, in love, or in law. Others, are more dextrous,

and with great art will lie on the watch to hook in their own praise.

And he is very negative about interruptions (Chapter 6):

There are two faults in conversation which appear very different, yet arise from the same root, and are equally blamable; I mean an impatience to interrupt others; and the uneasiness of being interrupted ourselves.

He explains:

The two chief ends of conversation are to entertain and improve those we are among, or to receive those benefits ourselves; which whoever will consider, cannot easily run into either of those two errours; because when any man speaks in company, it is to be supposed he does it for his hearers sake, and not his own; so that common discretion will teach us not to force their attention, if they are not willing to lend it; nor, on the other side, to interrupt him who is in possession, because that is in the grossest manner to give the preference to our own good sense.

The essay should be better known (it is available online in sites dedicated to Swift's writings), for it shows how little has changed over the past 300 years.

The way we talk about unhappy conversations has changed, though. Modern idiom provides us with several expressions that show problems of collaboration have occurred. Monopolizing, for example, tends to be acknowledged after the event:

I couldn't get a word in edgeways.
He went on and on about it.
She never said a word all evening.
A: Why didn't you say anything? B: I didn't get the chance.
They wouldn't stop talking shop.

Likewise, reaching an impasse:

I couldn't seem to get through to her.
He didn't take the hint.
It was like talking to a brick wall.

However, an underlying malaise can break out into an explicit
confrontation:

You never listen to a word I say.
Who do you think you are?
Why are you talking to me like that?
That's a bit rude, isn't it?
That's an awful thing to say!

An underlying confusion can become apparent:

I never said any such thing.
That's not what I said.
I didn't mean...
Did I say that?
What I'm trying to say is...
I think we're at cross purposes.
My point is...

And embarrassment, a sense of inappropriateness, or the desire to
avoid a painful personal allusion can be expressed too:

Can we change the subject?
I'd rather not go down that road.
I don't know what to say...

The alternative to these markers of conversational distress is the
least desirable outcome: silence, the ultimate signal of a failed conversation. In its extreme form it carries over into a ban on any further conversation: the people 'aren't speaking to each other'.

Of course, in real life, the people may not want to speak to each
other at all, and some writers provide self-help. This is Eugene
Mirman's solution, in *The Will to Whatevs: a Guide to Modern Life*
(2009):

Of course, to avoid getting stuck in that convo with someone you dislike or feel uncomfortable around, don't be passive, be pro-active. Do not let them direct your interaction on their terms, do it on yours. Ask a Misdirection Question—something too difficult to answer quickly—e.g., 'What's Congress up to?' or 'You ever learn any cool science?' When you ask the question, don't make eye contact, keep moving and get out of there. Do not wait for a response and deny ever asking it. Repeat these actions until you are never again spoken to by that individual (about four times).

I've never tried it, but it feels as if it ought to work.

Middles: going well

Ironically, there are far fewer explicit expressions of praise that participants use when a conversation is going well. Perhaps this isn't surprising. If all is well, what need to say so? In the 40 minutes of conversation transcribed in *Advanced Conversational English*, there are just the following instances of positive reinforcement:

you're quite right /
that's right /
that's a point /
I can imagine /
well there you are / you see /
you remember? /
that's good /
clever /
I quite agree with that /
I think you are /
very true /
I'm sure it does /
I suppose so /

There are no vivid metaphorical acknowledgements of the 'brick wall' kind. Indeed, most of the items are so predictable that they might be called clichés.

Similarly, there were hardly any examples of disagreement, and when they arose they were intonationally gentle and self-effacing:

oh I don't know about that /
oh come on /
really ? /

The few instances of uncertainty were deflected by questions or questioning intonations (the question mark shows a high rising tone):

is that what you mean ? /
you know what I mean ? /
you mean ? /

If there are so few explicit indicators of collaboration, how do people give positive reinforcement to each other while a conversation is proceeding? We have seen one answer to this question in Chapter 5: simultaneous feedback—*yeah, mm*, laughter, and so on. But there are many other cues.

Accommodation
People who are getting on well accommodate to each other's behaviour. They may sit in a similar way, or use similar body language. I don't have any records of that, as my recordings were audio only, but there are clear signs of accommodation throughout in the form of shared laughter, mimicking a tone of voice, adopting similar levels of loudness or speech rate, and overlapping the ends of each other's sentences (p. 41). One speaker adopts a confidential tone, and this causes others to do the same in their response. In this exchange, Dave has just mentioned how he would love a beer. Ed's wife responds:

EMMA [*whispers*]: don't talk so loud / Ed might hear you /
DAVE [*whispers*]: sorry / I'd love a beer /
ED: I heard that /

Comment clauses
The use of self-effacing comment clauses, of the kind I described in Chapter 8, beginning or ending a statement that otherwise might sound abrupt or pontificating:

it seems to me / it's a confession of a lack of a story /
I mean they're just not frank about it /
it's only what you'd expect / I suppose /

If you read these sentences again without the comment clause, you'll feel how the softening effect is lost.

Tag questions

The use of tag questions, especially with a falling intonation (they are 'telling', not 'asking'). Their function is to make an 'offering' of the utterance to the listener—another sign of the desire for collaboration.

A: it's a sure sign of failure / isn't it /
B: yeah /

A: you could have Christmas cake for brunch / còuldn't you /
B: yes /

These are very common, and sometimes occur in pairs, as in this sequence (about pigs):

A: they were horrible filthy snorting things / weren't they /
B: they are revolting / aren't they /

Similar in function are end-placed triggers that invite a response—*wouldn't you say?*, *don't you think?*—along with independent questions such as *what do you think?* and *do you agree?*

Uptalk

The use of a high rising tone on statements. Often called 'uptalk', it's used as a comprehension check:

o I've been reading some Evelyn Wàugh / – with a falling tone = 'I'm telling you'
o I've been reading some Evelyn Wáugh / – with a high rising tone = 'I'm asking if you know who Evelyn Waugh is'

Its value lies in its succinctness: it allows us to make a statement and ask a question at the same time, as in the Waugh example—the equivalent of an unspoken question: 'Do you know what I'm talking about?' If you do know, you'll simply nod and let me continue. If you don't, my intonation offers you a chance to get clarification ('Who's he?', 'Which book?'), as my utterance will be followed by a pause, along with an appropriately questioning facial expression. I don't need to spell out the options. If there are several people in the conversation, I'm giving everyone a chance to intervene.

Uptalk has an important social role, therefore, as it's an easy way of establishing social bonding and rapport. It shows that the speaker is thinking of the listener's needs. If I use it, I assume you know what I'm talking about, so we must know each other quite well, or at least have a shared background. Among a group of friends who share a social milieu, each instance of a rising tone on a statement says, in effect: 'Of course you know what I'm talking about, because we're mates.' That's probably the main reason it caught on so much among teenagers: it affirmed, in a trim and easy way, mutual recognition and acceptance as members of a peer group. At first it was largely heard among young women—an example of the way women usually take the lead in introducing linguistic change (p. 171)—but then it spread to young men, and since has been steadily working its way up the age range.

Uptalk became increasingly noticed during the late 1970s in New Zealand and Australia, and in the UK came to the attention of a wider audience a few years later through the Australian soap *Neighbours*. But British people were already familiar with uptalk because of American media, where it had been around from at least the days of the Californian hippies in the 1960s (you know?). And in Britain it had an even longer history, for several regional accents of the British Isles have always been associated with a rising lilt on statements, especially in Celtic-speaking areas. When people describe, say, the Welsh accent as 'musical', that's what they're noticing. We hear it strongly in Scotland and Northern Ireland too. And in view of the known presence of Celtic speakers of English among the first immigrants to Australia, that's maybe how it got into the Antipodean accent in the first place.

There are few references to uptalk in earlier periods of English, but the writer Joshua Steele does refer to it in his *Melody and Measure of Speech* (1775): he describes how many speakers offend by 'keeping up their [sentence] ends too high'. This is the first reference I know of uptalk being criticized. It can still generate antipathy, especially from older people. If overused, it can cause listener irritation: not everyone appreciates speakers who repeatedly suggest 'are you with me?' in their intonation. But its spread since the 1980s has been one of the most noticeable changes in English conversational practice. There's hardly any sign of it in my 1970s recordings, but I doubt it would be possible to find conversations today, especially among young people, that didn't display copious instances.

Keeping it going

Learning how to develop a point and how to keep it going is one of the first things we learn as a child, after turn-taking (p. 37). In its earliest guise, it takes the form of what studies of child language acquisition call *expansion*. Here's an example between a mother and her 2-year-old. They are looking at an animal picture-book. The child turns over a page:

CHILD: cow
MOTHER: no, that's not a cow / – that's an elephant /
CHILD: elephant /
MOTHER: he's very big / isn't he / – and look / he's got a long nose /
CHILD: got long nose /
MOTHER: yes / he's got a long nose / and d'you know what it's called / his nose /
CHILD: *shakes head*
MOTHER: it's called a trunk / – can you say trunk /
CHILD: trunk /
MOTHER: a big long trunk /

What the mother is doing, systematically yet unconsciously, is expanding her child's utterances. She is simultaneously teaching new vocabulary and new grammar (such as how to use two adjectives before a noun). In effect she's saying to the child: this is what you've said about this topic; and this is something else you could have said. One day, this child will answer a question about an elephant in a very different way, such as:

Q: what's an elephant /
A: an elephant is a large animal with a big long trunk /

But it will take several intermediate stages of language learning to reach that point.

With adults we can see a similar process of expansion taking the conversation forward. One speaker says 'X is a problem', and the other takes up the cue with some such response as

yes it's an enormous problem /
and especially a problem where I live /

Often the process is not so much one of expansion as of reformulation:

it's a real difficulty / actually /

or the introduction of a related topic:

I've seen a similar situation where I live /
I can give you an instance of that /

In more thoughtful settings, the speaker can try to plan ahead:

I'd make two points about that /

though in the give-and-take of a multi-party conversation, the risk is always that other interventions will mean that the second point will never be made, or have to be brought up again later when there's an appropriate gap in the conversation (and the speaker seizes the opportunity: 'That's the other thing I was going to say…'). This is one of the big differences between conversation and the structured interactions of debates or committee meetings, where forward planning is respected, and may be highly sophisticated. I actually once heard an observer at a board meeting, who had hitherto been silent, respond to an invitation to contribute by saying: 'I have eighteen points I want to make'—*and* he made them!

Endings

There are two types of ending within a conversation: we need a way of showing we want to end a topic, if there is more than one, and we need a way of showing we want to end the entire conversational event. The first is easy; the second trickier.

The content will often dictate the first. A joke will have a punchline, a story will have some sort of climax. But if there is no intrinsic semantic signpost, the fact that speakers have reached the end of what they wanted to say on a topic may need to be explicitly marked. Sometimes the markers draw attention directly to the moment:

> ... right / that's me done / ---
> ... I've said enough about that / ---
> ... let's move on / ---
> ... so I suppose there's nothing more to be said / ---

In more formal settings, there may be a *finally*, *lastly*, or suchlike to act as a signpost. In informal settings, the markers are more often indirect, even to the point of cliché:

> ... so it goes / ---
> ... it makes you think / doesn't it / ---
> ... that's life / I suppose / ---
> ... and then it disappeared / so --- [*with elongated vowel*: sooo]

They may also be lexically inexplicit: we sense a topic is coming to a close if the speaker noticeably slows down, lowers voice, and introduces a longer pause than normal. A final *but er*—or *so* (p. 177)—is often enough. There may be non-linguistic cues in the form of pursed lips, looking away from the other participants, or a body movement, such as a shrug of the shoulders. In the Gerry/Tony conversation, one end-of-topic moment was signalled by Tony picking up a sandwich and starting to eat it. Listeners then have to choose—whether to respect the speaker's choice or to continue the topic for themselves, breathing new life into it. If someone comes out with an *mmm*, it suggests that he/she doesn't want to speak next.

The trickier situation occurs when participants realize that their conversation is coming to an end. When the conversation is between passers-by, a simple *must be going, must get back to work, gosh look at the time, have to run, nice talking to you, lovely chat, mustn't keep you,* and the like, will suffice to indicate that there is a desire for closure. There may be accompanying non-linguistic behaviour, such as looking at a watch. It isn't always easy, as a character in Haruki Murakami's short story 'Hunting Knife' (2006) finds:

> He was silent for thirty seconds, maybe a minute. I uncrossed my legs under the table and wondered if this was the right moment to leave. It was as if my whole life revolved around trying to judge the right point in a conversation to say goodbye.

A rather different situation obtains at the end of a conversation between hosts and guests, when the visitors feel it's time to leave. The following exchange would be totally unacceptable:

> HOST [*reaching the end of a story*]: . . . so I won't be doing that sort of thing again in a hurry / [*pause*]
> GUEST: well, I must be going /
> *GUEST stands up and leaves the room*

What actually happens is something like this:

> GUEST: Well, this has been really lovely. Time to go back to the cats, I suppose.
> HOST: It's been great. Thanks so much for coming over.
> *But nobody moves, and a new topic of conversation is introduced, about the cats, which goes on for another five minutes or so. Then there's another pause.*

GUEST: Well, we really must be going. [*Stands up.*]
HOST [*also stands up*]: We must do it again...[*They leave the room.*]

The expectation is that the guest(s) give an early warning of closure, which is then followed, a short time later, by a repeat of the desire to close. Just one repetition suffices. It's unusual to hear a 'we must go' type of expression being said a third or fourth time, after further pauses and continuations.

Underlying all the examples in this chapter is a concern to provide the participants in a conversation with linguistic clues to let everyone know whether things are going successfully. These clues are not only there to aid the listener; they benefit the speaker too. And they come into their own when people tell each other stories.

Phone beginnings

How to start a call was hugely controversial in the early days of telephony (p. 42). There was clearly a need to say something when answering a call, but what? Alexander Graham Bell opted for *Ahoy*. Edison went for *Hello*. Other contenders were *Hulloa!* and *I am here*. The manual issued by the first public exchange, which opened in New Haven in January 1878, suggested both *Hello* and *What is wanted?*

Hello won, despite the fact that it had not long been in the language. It's first recorded in 1826–7 as a word used to attract attention or express surprise, but it didn't emerge as a greeting until the 1850s. It became so popular that by 1883 the female telephone operators were being colloquially referred to as 'hello girls'. By the 1920s, the practice was so routine that some manuals recommended dropping it entirely as unnecessary. Apart from anything else, it was thought, long sequences of people at both ends saying *hello* took up too much time.

Then there was the question of identifying yourself. Who should name themselves first? In August 1905 an issue of the *Madera Mercury*, a newspaper in California, commented on etiquette:

> good manners make it necessary for the one calling to introduce one's self before engaging in conversation. Some illbred people have the vulgarity and impudence to try to compel the party called to give his or her name first.

Today, what happens? *Hello* is still widely used, but according to a 2008 survey by the Post Office in the UK, a third of young people aged 18 to 24 now answer their (mobile) phones with a *hi, yo, whassup,* or some other colloquial expression. The practice of responding with a number or name also seems to be dying out, chiefly because caller ID is now routinely visible, so there's no longer any need to say who's picked up the phone. And that's led to a new practice: if I know it's Wendy who is calling, I can now answer by saying *Hi Wendy*. The Victorians would have thought this was witchcraft.

Chapter Ten

STORY-TELLING

Although conversation is defined as a dialogue, in practice it's often more like a series of monologues, linked by the occasional acknowledgement or reaction, and accompanied by copious simultaneous feedback (p. 38). We saw this at the beginning of Chapter 8, in the Gerry and Tony conversation, where each of them at a certain point launches into an extended account of an issue. This is typical of the genre, whatever the topic and regardless of the relationship between the participants. It will be seen in a scholarly discussion of an intellectual topic, as well as in a gossipy chat about neighbourhood affairs. A conversation in which people tell each other jokes is, I suppose, the clearest example of a monologue chain. But monologues will characterize any occasion in which we tell stories—about our holidays, a shopping trip, a hospital visit, an episode on TV, a football game...—or respond to an information question with a lengthy exposition.

Few people consider themselves eloquent, but we only have to listen to someone telling such stories to realize that most are, actually, naturally eloquent. Humans are born story-tellers, and we learn to gossip, tell jokes, repeat stories, and recount what has happened to us without reflecting on the fluency involved. The self-doubt comes when we think of ourselves having to tell our stories in public, with an audience, in the form of a speech. Five-year-olds have no such inhibitions. I have a recording of Suzie at that age who retells the story of 'The Three Little Pigs' to a group of adults, and it goes on for over two minutes. Admittedly it was full of hesitations, repetitions, and immaturities, but it was an impressive performance nonetheless. And parents will be very familiar with the unceasing monologues that accompany a child of that age (often younger) playing happily with a pile of toys, and making up a story about them.

When we launch into a story, we have to do several things at once. We need to maintain a smooth continuity in what we're saying, avoiding the kind of mental disruption that forces us to backtrack ('Oh I forgot to say…') or ask for help ('What was I saying?', 'Where was I?'). We need to keep our listeners interested. And we need to make our discourse comfortable—which means for the speaker as well as for the listener. We achieve all three ends by using quite a small number of linguistic strategies.

Maintaining continuity

In the previous chapter I described some of the ways in which speakers collaborate to keep a conversation going. At the same time as all those interactional strategies are being used, there is also the basic linguistic need to preserve continuity. All stories require that sentences be joined together to form a discourse. How is that done?

The basic narrative technique is simple addition: the use of the conjunction *and*, often reinforced by a time word, *then*. *And* is simply a plus sign, distributing the emphasis evenly throughout the utterance. It adds nothing to the meaning of the linked structures—unlike *or*, for example, which expresses an alternative, or *but*, which expresses a contrast. *And* is far and away the commonest connective. The whole of the 'driving' story (Recording 5) contains 45 main clauses: 29 of them (two-thirds) are linked by *and*. Some of them are illustrated in the extract on p. 102 below. It's a connectivity strategy that is the first to be learned by children, at around age 3, and it stays with us all our lives. (This narrative pattern is well known to primary school teachers, who note its frequency in the early connected writing of their pupils, and try to get them to replace it with more sophisticated forms of sentence connection. But it never entirely leaves us, and readily resurfaces in informal letter writing, blogs, and other informal Internet exchanges.)

The pattern 'this happened and then this happened and then this happened...' is the underlying structure of narrative, but we can easily imagine that an entire story constructed only in this way would sound boring. To avoid this, we add to this pattern in various ways, introducing further connecting expressions.

- We can reinforce or supplement the meaning of what we've just said by repeating it, paraphrasing it, or adding a fresh piece of information about it. Connectives of this kind include *as a matter of fact, in other words, as I say, that is, really, for instance.*

- We can diminish or retract the meaning of what we've just said. Connectives of this kind include *at least, or rather, at any rate,* and *actually.*

- We can give our story a fresh direction, or a new level of organization. Connectives of this kind include *the trouble is, the point is, the thing is,* and so on, as well as such words and phrases as *so, anyway, in a nutshell, all in all, to cut a long story short,* and *on the whole.* In effect, we're saying to our listener: 'Never mind what I've said about this so far, the main point I want you to focus on is the following.'

When I say 'we repeat ourselves', I don't mean the same words are repeated exactly. The precise repetition of an utterance is likely to occur only in arguments or in extremely insistent situations ('I want to go. I want to go. How many times must I keep on saying it?') or where a very specific rhetorical point is being made (as in Barack Obama's repeated 'Yes we can' in his 2008 victory address). The kind of thing that usually happens can be illustrated by these extracts from the *Advanced Conversational English* recordings.

you can go to a nightclub / in Birmingham / – and watch Tony Bennett / . for about thirty bob / – something like this / a night with Tony Bennett / –

> as long as one is careful / – very careful / it's all right /
> I ban all bangers / . we don't have any bangers /

These are all examples of a single repetition. This next extract shows a double one:

> I don't know where we can get any wood from / apart from chop-
> ping down a few trees / which I wouldn't like to do / – we don't seem
> to have very much wood / – well I suppose if we went into the park
> / we might collect a few sticks / but it's not quite like having . logs /
> is it / – but I don't know where one would get this from here /

This is absolutely normal conversational practice. What is unusual is to see it in public speaking situations, such as a political speech, where a more crafted and more formal discourse has been the norm:

> I inherited a mess. It's a mess. At home and abroad, a mess.

The repetitiveness heard in Donald Trump's speeches has been much commented upon; but all he is doing is tapping into a conversational style that—whatever his critics say—evidently resonates with large numbers of voters. 'He talks like us.'

Adding interest

Another way of avoiding the potential mundane nature of an under-lying 'and then' narrative is to add extra interest to the story while it unfolds. Dramatic adjectives and adverbs are especially important. Adjective sequences are common:

> have a nice meal / . in . very . plushy surroundings / very warm /
> nice / pleasant / – says it costs him / about the same amount of
> money / to go and sit in a breezy windy stand / – on a . on a
> wooden bench / . . .

Intensifying words are especially popular, adding emphasis, but seman-tically non-specific other than expressing a very general positive or negative emotion:

we had super weather / – absolutely super /
oh it was fantastic / the speed that they got out /

The adverbs are often a replacement for the general-purpose *very*:

how absolutely lovely it is /
it can get fearfully dull /
extraordinarily expensive shops /

English has a large number of such adjectives and adverbs—*marvel-lous, smashing, superb, wonderful, great, awful, grotty, revolting, rubbish, yucky*...—though they are subject to social change. One generation's *smashing* is the next generation's *stunning*. And personality enters into it too: people have their favourite intensifiers.

Semantically more specific adjectives and adverbs can be seen in these examples:

I remember / there was a terrible story / – horrifying story / that was told by a colleague of mine / ...
Leeds played shockingly / – worst game they ever played /
newspapers / were absolutely infuriating /

The overall impression is one of rhetorical exaggeration, which affects nouns too:

they found hordes of children / who wanted these pets /
we were reaching a stage of hysteria /
there were masses of them /

Comfortable discourse

The notion of conversational comfort has two dimensions: the lis-tener needs to feel comfortable, and so does the speaker. An expres-sion such as *in a nutshell* benefits listeners, as it helps them follow the way the conversation is going; but it also benefits speakers, as it gives them an opportunity to think about where they want the conversation to go next. For listeners, these expressions act as 'signposts'; for speakers, more as 'breathing points'.

The 'signpost' metaphor is slightly misleading in one respect. Like the roadside signpost, a linguistic pointer turns up at a place where the speaker is choosing a particular direction for the next stage of the journey. But on the road there might be miles between one signpost and the next; whereas in conversations, the linguistic equivalent turns up, as it were, every few yards. We frequently check that our story is going well, using the collaborative expressions I described in the previous chapter and the connectivity markers described above.

We don't notice their frequency unless one particular signpost is used without variation—such as someone who repeatedly says *OK?* or (the *bête noire* of the new millennium) *like*. Then it draws attention to itself, and can distract from what's being said. But usually we introduce a diversity of signposts into our narratives; and their frequency isn't noticed because of the way our discourse is structured.

We break our speech up into short rhythmical and intonational chunks. This is how one story-teller in *Advanced Conversational English* (Recording 5) does it. He's recalling an unfortunate driving incident. As with earlier extracts, the rhythm units are demarcated by a forward slash, and pauses by a dot (short) or a dash (longer); simultaneous feedback is omitted.

> and – he backed it / out of the garage / so that it was standing on the driveway / – and he'd closed the garage doors / – and – she came out of the house / – to . take this car out / and go shopping for the first time / – so she came out / very gingerly / – and opened the door / . and sat in the car / – and er . began to back / . very very gently / – taking . great care you see / that she didn't do anything to this . to this new car / – and – as she backed / – there was an unpleasant crunching sound / . . .

There are 457 words in the whole story, and the average number of words per rhythm unit is 5.02. In Tony's 386-word story (Recording 1), it is 4.88. In another 277-word story (Recording 12), it is 5.1. If I did the same count for all the recordings in the book, the results would be similar. The average number of words per rhythm unit would be around 5. This fits in perfectly with the experimental findings in psycholinguistics which suggest that this is an especially comfortable length for the brain to process—a research field that began with a famous article by American psychologist George Miller called 'The magic number seven, plus or minus two: some limits on our capacity for processing information' (1956). Story-tellers seem to gravitate naturally towards it, because it helps both them and their listeners.

The boundaries of these rhythm units are the places where breathing points (metaphorical, and sometimes physical) most naturally fall. In the driving story, the speaker has reached a dramatic moment, and evidently feels that the pauses between the units are enough to help us process the sequence of events comfortably. He's also speaking quite slowly. By contrast, this next speaker (in Recording 3) is talking rapidly and enthusiastically; the average rhythm unit length (ignoring hesitations) is as expected, in the normal range (4.8), but there are fewer pauses, and explicit signposts are more in evidence (underlined):

> it's just misrepresentation / because . erm <u>obviously I mean</u> /
> when there wa was this assassination attempt / - erm there was -
> some tension in Cyprus / it would be childish / to say there
> wasn't / - but people went on living quite normally / . and er it
> wasn't really such a serious matter / <u>I mean</u> fortunately / he
> wasn't shot / and <u>that was that</u> / <u>you see</u> / <u>I mean</u> w that's how
> most pe people took it / and erm so many other cases / <u>as well</u> /
> where there've been - erm international situations / that erm -
> people re . have really just taken as part of their normal life / and
> it hasn't affected / the everyday life of Cyprus / at all / . <u>you know</u> /

There's a tendency to play down the significance of comment clauses such as *you know, you see,* and *I mean.* They are often viewed as signs of non-fluency—and indeed, if overused, or used inappropriately (as in a radio interview), they deserve their bad press.

But in most everyday conversations their presence passes unnoticed. In fact, if they weren't there, we would feel uneasy. A dimension of spontaneous informality would be missing. There's a big difference between

> *A* I mean that's how most people took it

and

> *B* that's how most people took it

or between

> *A* it hasn't affected / the everyday life of Cyprus / at all / . you know /

and

> *B* it hasn't affected / the everyday life of Cyprus / at all /

The difference is stylistic: the comment clauses soften the force of the *A* sentences; by contrast, the *B* sentences sound more abrupt or authoritative. In the *B* sentences, the speaker is telling his listeners what was the case, and not offering them any say in the matter; in the *A* sentences, he is suggesting it, and his listeners have the option of taking him up on the point. Stylistic variation is a critical consideration in conversation analysis, and it turns out that there are more ways of varying our style than we might expect.

A thousand days

Here's the beginning of Suzie's story of 'The Three Little Pigs' (p. 97):

> One – one day they went out to build their houses. One built it of
> straw, one built it of sticks, and one built it of bricks. And he –
> the little busy brother knowed that in the woods there lived a big
> bad wolf, he need nothing else but to catch little pigs. So you
> know what, one day they went out – and – the wolf went slip slosh
> slip slosh went his feet on the ground...

The 'and then' pattern is there, but there is one feature of this monologue which shows that she is quite advanced for her age: 'you know
what'. Children don't normally use comment clauses and connecting adverbials (such as *you see*, *actually*, *fortunately*) until much older.
They start to appear sporadically around age 7, but their frequency
and distribution don't reflect adult norms until after age 10.

Interactive expressions, especially expressing politeness, are much
earlier, because parents drill them. A typical dialogue at around age 3
would go like this:

> CHILD: Can I have another biscuit?
> PARENT: I haven't heard that little word yet!
> CHILD: Can I have another biscuit, PLEASE.
> PARENT: That's better.

Why 3? Because this is the stage where the main sentence structures
are well established, pronunciation is intelligible, and quite a large
vocabulary—around 3000 words—has been acquired. It's now possible to have reasonably sophisticated conversations, so that, from a
parent's point of view, the basic challenges of language learning

seem to have been met. The language now needs 'polishing', by introducing the child to the rules of polite interaction. It's an age where we hear, in parent–child conversations, such advice about what *not* to say as well as how to say it:

Don't talk with your mouth full.

You mustn't say that naughty word.

Say please.

Thank you. [*said by the parent to a child who has remained silent after just having been given something*]

Age 3 is also the time most children begin joining phrases and sentences together with *and*. The basic narrative strategy emerges. It's a remarkable achievement, really, when we reflect that these little beings have been on earth for only a thousand days.

Chapter Eleven

STYLISTIC OPTIONS

> Like other parties of the kind, it was first silent, then talky, then
> argumentative, then disputatious, then unintelligible, then alto-
> gethery, then inarticulate, and then drunk.

This was Lord Byron, writing in 1815 to his friend Thomas Moore
after a dinner party the day before. It's as close as anyone has got to
reporting one of the most important characteristics of conversation:
its stylistic unpredictability. It would have been no good asking
Byron to describe the style—or even the content—in greater detail.
He added:

> I carried away much wine, and the wine had previously carried
> away my memory; so that all was hiccup and happiness for
> the last hour or so, and I am not impregnated with any of the
> conversation.

For such descriptions, we need sober stylisticians.

It might be thought that unpredictability of style is simply a reflection of the topic shifts I described in Chapter 7, but there is far more
to it. We come to a conversation with several stylistic options, and
our choice of these is influenced by the number of people taking
part, the nature of their relationship, their expectations (if any)
about the outcome, the setting in which they're talking, and the constraints (such as limited time) they have to respect—not forgetting,
evidently, how much they've had to drink.

How are these stylistic variables to be described? A useful approach is through the notion of *collocation*—words that commonly 'go together'—and especially the adjectives that people most often use in everyday speech to talk about a conversation. We can think of it like this: what items can fill the blank in the sentence: *We had a(n)— conversation?* I've brought together over a hundred, and grouped them into five categories: formality, depth, distance, enjoyment, and amusement.

Formality

The stylistic feature most often mentioned in grammars, dictionaries, and English-teaching textbooks is *formality*. At the Byron dinner, the evening seems to have been formal to begin with, given the persons 'of note and notoriety' (as he describes them) who were there, but it soon became informal. The relationship between the two is actually a spectrum.

```
most formal <--------------------------------> most informal
```

Adjectives that suggest informality include *casual, ordinary, everyday, domestic, personal,* and *family*; formal situations might be described as *solemn, stiff, mannered, courteous, official,* or *polite*. The degree of formality can in principle be quantified by noting the number of relevant features of pronunciation, orthography, grammar, and vocabulary that the participants use, as in these examples:

Informal	Formal
whaddaya mean?	what do you mean?
this shouldn't be seen as...	this should not be seen as...
expect to arrive on Thursday	we expect to arrive on Thursday
we did good	we did well
start	commence
nope	no

The use of a very frequent feature, such as contracted verb forms (*I'm, they're, isn't, won't...*), will immediately identify speech (or writing) as informal; and their absence will convey the opposite. Similarly, informal speech is going to contain many slang expressions, changes in naming (*David > Dave*), loosely linked constructions, incomplete sentences, comment clauses, and so on, which will either have their equivalent in formal settings or be avoided altogether. It will also show a more erratic prosodic organization: the units of rhythm/intonation will be shorter and more uneven. Here's an example from the beginning of the Gerry/Tony conversation—first, the speech as it occurred, and then one possible formal rendition, showing more complex syntax, and longer and more balanced rhythm units:

> I was reading in the paper this morning / a a chap / he's a director / of a big company / in Birmingham /
>
> I was reading in the paper this morning / about a gentleman who is a director of a big company in Birmingham /

All the recordings in *Advanced Conversational English* were from informal situations where the participants knew each other. Even so, the level of informality varied between conversations, as some of them were close friends, in regular touch, while others had not been in contact for quite a while.

An individual conversation can vary too. One that starts informally (or formally) will normally finish informally (or formally), and that was certainly the case with all the ones I recorded. But there were moments when the tone shifted. Take this sentence:

> in what way have conditions deteriorated /

Out of context, we would immediately say this was a formal way of asking the question—more likely to occur, for instance, in an interview between people who didn't know each other. In fact it's in the middle of the Gerry/Tony conversation, which is otherwise totally informal. Tony might have asked the question in a less formal way ('how've conditions deteriorated?'), but—presumably because he wanted the topic to be treated in greater depth—he decided to inject a hint of seriousness into the dialogue.

In many accounts of conversation, formality is the only stylistic feature referred to. But there are several other variables which contribute to the way the tone or mood of a conversation is maintained or alters, and which would influence our opinion about its quality, were someone to ask us after it was over: 'How did it go?'

Depth

How did it go? We might think of the level of informativeness with which we treated a topic, such as health, sport, issues at work, or domestic problems. If we've explored it in some depth, we would use that metaphor, and talk about having had a *deep* conversation, or we might say we had a *real, serious, thoughtful, reflective, sophisticated, intelligent, meaningful, learnèd, scholarly* conversation. Such talk would have been characterized by precision and technicality, especially if some of us were 'talking shop' at some point. Conversely, we would describe it as a *shallow* conversation if the topic had been treated in a *superficial, frivolous, perfunctory, lightweight* manner, and here we would have used approximation and vagueness.

None of this should be taken as a criticism. A superficial treatment of a topic can be all that is needed, as in this exchange between colleagues:

how was the meeting?
oh fine / - nothing to write home about / - same old same old /

or this one between spouses:

what did you get?
the usual / - tomatoes / cheese / crisps /

Sufficient for the day is the vagueness thereof, where a greater amount of information is unnecessary. Of course, if there has been some misjudgement between the speakers about the level of depth required, it will be followed up with a request for more precision.

If the topic is at all contentious, such as religion and politics, then we can use a further set of adjectives to describe the depth achieved, such as *adult, mature, real-life, grown-up,* and *civilized,* with its opposites including *childish, puerile, juvenile,* and *infantile.* If the topic is sex, yet another lexical domain opens up: the conversation can now be *dirty, bawdy, coarse, filthy, indelicate, indecent, smutty, crude,* and there may be requests (jocular or serious) to 'keep the conversation clean'.

Distance

How did it go? We might think of the level of closeness, or intimacy, that existed between us—how well we knew each other and how far we were prepared to reveal our thoughts and feelings to each other. This would affect both what we talked about as well as what we didn't talk about. The quotation from Oliver Wendell Holmes in my Prologue is relevant here: 'The whole force of conversation depends on how much you can take for granted.' When a conversation is private, we talk about it as being *intimate, close, confidential, personal, discreet, quiet*—or not so quiet, if that is how we interpret Byron's *altogethery.* If there's a lack or loss of intimacy, we would use such words as *distant, strange, cool, frigid, icy, reserved.* An entire conversation might be described in these terms.

Because the nature of the relationship between participants is a constant, we might not expect intimacy to vary at all within a conversation where the number of people stays the same throughout. But there can be moments when the level of intimacy changes, and language provides us with cues to let others know that this is about to happen. The switch is invariably from a *public* to a *private* (or mock-private) conversation, signalled by an introductory formula such as *just between you and me* and *off the record.* There will be a noticeable alteration in tone—typically a lowering of the loudness level, an alteration in speech rate, and a different tone of voice, which in the most dramatic situations emerges as the archetypal case of confidentiality, a whisper. Or mock-confidentiality, as in the whispered exchange reported on p. 87.

The reason we switch from public to private, rather than the other way round, is because conversations are in principle hospitable; it is intimacy that is the special case. If two people are having a conversation, and another wants to join in—an acquaintance coming up in a bar, a guest arriving at a party, a family member joining others in a sitting room—there is nothing to prevent this happening other than the usual phatic pleasantries, such as 'Mind if I join you?' And there is in theory no limit to the number of participants that might be welcomed into a conversation—though if the number is larger than four, it proves difficult to manage, and within-group conversations arise. Ralph Waldo Emerson noted the phenomenon, in *Society and Solitude* (1870):

> Put any company of people together with freedom for conversation, and a rapid self-distribution takes place into sets and pairs.

He memorably concluded: 'All conversation is a magnetic experiment.'

Enjoyment

'How did it go?' We may remember the conversation simply because it was *friendly, warm, relaxed, laid-back, easy-going, pleasant, lovely, agreeable, fascinating, good*: in short, 'we enjoyed it'. Or the opposite: we remember it as *tense, difficult, trying, awkward, cool, prickly, strained, stressful, stilted, uncomfortable*: in short, 'we didn't enjoy it'. Here too, the event may vary, and participants may recall a conversation in different ways. A conversation might start by being relaxed and end up awkward, or vice versa, or there may be several such changes of atmosphere in between. Paul Auster in his novel *Moon Palace* (1989) describes precisely such a change, and in his own vivid way hints at some of the stylistic features that identify it:

Bit by bit, I found myself relaxing into the conversation. Kitty had a natural talent for drawing people out of themselves, and it was easy to fall in with her, to feel comfortable in her presence. As Uncle Victor had once told me long ago, a conversation is like having a catch with someone. A good partner tosses the ball directly into your glove, making it almost impossible for you to miss it; when he is on the receiving end, he catches everything sent his way, even the most errant and incompetent throws. That's what Kitty did. She kept lobbing the ball straight into the pocket of my glove, and when I threw the ball back to her, she hauled in everything that was even remotely in her area: jumping up to spear balls that soared above her head, diving nimbly to her left or right, charging in to make tumbling, shoestring catches. More than that, her skill was such that she always made me feel that I had made those bad throws on purpose, as if my only object had been to make the game more amusing. She made me seem better than I was, and that strengthened my confidence, which in turn helped to make my throws less difficult for her to handle. In other words, I started talking to her rather than to myself, and the pleasure of it was greater than anything I had experienced in a long time.

There are many reasons for enjoyment. We might simply have taken pleasure in the liveliness of the conversation, describing it as *animated, spirited, upbeat, earnest, passionate, enthusiastic.* Conversely, we might simply feel it was *boring, tedious, dull, lifeless,* or dismiss the occasion out of hand with words like *ridiculous, inane, nonsensical, absurd.* If the aim of the conversation was to bring something out into the open, then we would encounter such adjectives as *honest, candid, frank, forthright, creative*; less successful outcomes would result in words like *tactful, respectful, civil, cautious, delicate, diplomatic,* with stronger items including *tough, blunt, heated, confrontational, contentious, bad-tempered, acrimonious.* If its aim was to be helpful in some way, then we would be more likely to hear *supportive, constructive, accommodating, cooperative, productive, useful, stimulating, worthwhile,* as opposed to *unhelpful, inconclusive, impossible, meaningless, idle, pointless, futile, purposeless, useless.* With adjectives like these, of course, we are encountering the style in which political diplomatic conversations are reported. This is the language of Brexit negotiations.

Amusement

'How did it go?' We may remember the conversation because it was *witty, amusing, jokey, light-hearted, silly, crazy,* on the one hand, or *serious, humourless, no-nonsense, weighty,* on the other. This is a dimension where there's a great deal of variation. Our impression that a conversation was amusing is based on many individual instances of amusement that took place. It's unlikely that the amusement was in evidence throughout the entire conversation (which would actually be rather wearing), and in every recording in *Advanced Conversational English* the occurrences were sporadic. But they were also extremely varied in their function.

What is the evidence for amusement? In a video recording, we would note smiles, grins, and head nods as positive signs, and frowns, scowls, and head-shakes as negative. For the audio recordings I had available, the clearest indications were giggles and laughs—or groans, after a pun—and virtually every recording was punctuated by laughter, usually a short pulse or two from listeners as they gave simultaneous feedback (p. 38). However, hardly any of these laughs were the result of someone deliberately being funny or telling a joke—a point that can surprise, as our normal expectation is that laughter is naturally associated with humour. Other factors were involved.

Here are some examples of the laughs heard in my recordings, along with an interpretation of their function. (L) marks the point in the speech where they occurred:

- the laugh showed appreciation of a piece of vivid phrasing
  - to go and sit in a breezy windy stand / (L)
  - there was an unpleasant crunching sound / (L)
  - they'd be off and away / little grey smooth sleeky things / (L)

- the laugh expressed sympathy or recognition
  - I didn't really enjoy the flames very much / (L)
  - well it (L) sounds a bit like / where we're living in a way /
- the laugh acknowledged the use of an emotive or sensitive word
  - paki bashing / (L) was – at its height / then /
- the laugh acknowledged a self-criticism
  - part of life if you like / makes it sound a bit pompous / (L)
- the laugh showed appreciation of an unexpected piece of precision
  - he's watched football in every league ground in England / all ninety two / (L)

These five factors—formality, depth, distance, enjoyment, amusement—by no means account for all the stylistic variations we encounter in conversations. We can talk about the content of a conversation as being *interesting* or *uninteresting*, with more emotive synonyms such as *riveting*, *enthralling*, and *fascinating* for the former, and *dull*, *boring*, and *tedious* for the latter. We can talk about them in terms of length: *brief*, *short*, *quick*, *fleeting*, *lengthy*, *long*, *endless*. . . , and sometimes can even quantify them: *hour-long*, *twenty-minute*. There may also be a time-frame implicit in the associated event, as when we talk about a *breakfast* conversation—or *lunchtime*, *dinnertime*, *cocktail-party*, *salon*, *bedtime*, *Saturday-night*. But this only adds to the main point being addressed in this chapter: that a great deal more is going on in them than is suggested by simple labels such as 'informal', which imply a homogeneity that just isn't there. All the conversations I've ever analysed have proved to be stylistically heterogeneous. There is never a guarantee that, just because a particular set of linguistic features is being used by the participants at any one point in a conversation, the same set will be observed a minute before or a minute after. There is indeed an underlying trend towards uniformity dictated by the constant elements in the social situation, but this is disrupted by unpredictable change. My recordings show several examples of changes taking place.

Altering a voice or a regional accent

A casual reference to a football team leads to someone adopting the voice of a well-known football commentator. A mother reports the way her child asked her for something and uses an immature child-speak intonation to do so. One participant tells a joke about an Englishman, an Irishman, and a Scotsman, and attempts the two Celtic accents at the relevant points in the story; others in the group take up the theme and play with the accents for a while.

Pun-capping

Someone inadvertently or deliberately makes a pun, and others in the group compete to find a better pun. One speaker coined the word *catfrontation* (for a confrontation in the street between two cats), and this led to a series of puns using the *cat-* prefix (a *catalogue* of disasters, one of the cats had *catarrh*, and so on) in a conversation that had previously not been noticeably jocular. The *cat* pun then recurred at intervals later in the conversation. I describe the whole event in the opening chapter of my *Language Play*.

Avoiding a misunderstanding

Several expressions identify a point in a conversation where one of the participants suddenly realizes it's going wrong and wants to get it back on track. They include *but seriously, it was a joke, don't take what I said personally, never mind that, I'm just kidding / teasing / joshing.*

Adopting an authoritative attitude

A fresh tone is immediately introduced when someone addresses a topic with the introductory formula *speaking as...* The selection can be serious (*speaking as a mother...*) or jocular (*speaking as someone who's never actually seen a ghost...*), and the reference can be to the speaker or to a listener: *speaking as someone whose face does resemble a Dalek* could be followed by any personal pronoun.

Changing pronouns

Alternations between *I, we,* and *one,* or between *he, she,* and *they* are often unpredictable. People can vacillate widely as they change their perspective, thinking of an event one moment as personal and the next moment as shared, or close to them and then distant. In my Recording 2, Mary wonders how to find wood for her bonfire. Based on her usage in the first 25 words of this example (up to *I don't know*), we would expect the pronoun in the last clause to be *I* or *we*—but we get *one*:

> I suppose if we went into the park / we might collect a few sticks / but it's not quite like having logs / is it / – but I don't know where one would get this from here /

This sort of thing would never be accepted in formal speech or in writing. Copy-editors would consistentize, as indeed do novelists, whose characters speak in a much more consistent way than real humans do. As Dr Johnson put it, in the *Adventurer* newspaper (28 August 1753):

> in conversation we naturally diffuse our thoughts, and in writing we contract them; method is the excellence of writing, and unconstraint the grace of conversation.

It is this lack of constraint that is the hallmark of a natural conversation—which is why feeding novels into a computer to improve its conversational skills, as Google did in 2016, is only going to go so far. It misses the point that conversations in novels are artistic constructs. If anyone were to write a novel that faithfully reflected the kind of stylistic variation and unpredictability we find in everyday conversation, I'm not sure it would be readable! The whole of the Gerry/Tony extract is reproduced as an Appendix to this book (p. 193). If this were an extract from a novel, I doubt you'd be salivating to find out what happened next.

This is the factor that programmers need to take on board if they are ever going to make their robots have a conversation that is genuinely human. The chatterbots I've heard in call centres, mobile apps, and virtual assistants (such as Siri and Alexa) all have a pedestrian predictability—well-articulated pronunciation, balanced prosody, carefully constructed sentence structure, precise vocabulary—that distances them from the kind of thing I've been describing in this book. Their function, of course, is primarily to provide information in response to questions, but that in itself is an unusual feature of everyday conversation, as Chapter 8 explained. Experiments have shown that it's possible for listeners to be unable to tell the difference between a machine-generated conversation and a human one (the Turing test). However, this result obtains only if the kind of conversation selected is of a certain type. No artificial intelligence (AI) device yet offers simultaneous feedback of the kind described in Chapter 5, or knows how to accommodate to sudden human stylistic shifts, or is able to make plausible stylistic shifts of its own. American journalist George Anders summed this up in an online *MIT Technology Review* essay on the Amazon chatterbot Alexa in 2017:

> The ultimate triumph for voice-based AI would be to carry on a realistic, multi-minute conversation with users. Such a feat will require huge jumps in machines' ability to discern human speakers' intent, even when there isn't an obvious request. Humans can figure out that a friend who says 'I haven't been to the gym in weeks' probably wants to talk about stress or self-esteem. For AI software, that's a hard leap. Sudden switches in topic—or oblique allusions—are tough, too.

We are light years away from the scenario of a robot with us in a room interacting conversationally by using all the techniques described so far in this book. Is this ever going to happen? The stylistic unpredictability that seems to be inherent in human interaction may be an impossible feature to simulate. But it is early days. The analysis of natural, spontaneous, everyday, domestic, informal conversation is in its infancy, and for a good reason: it is the most difficult domain of human linguistic behaviour to explore scientifically. Analysing authentic examples is relatively easy—once we have obtained reliable recordings, and that turns out to be hugely difficult. Yet I've been using examples of this genre throughout this book. How did I get them?

Hello, Dave

In all human–computer interactions I've read, it's assumed that both sides are competent communicators, and that this reflects real life. We see the early science in this field brought to life fictitiously in films such as *2001*, where HAL talks to astronaut Dave Bowman (p. 181), and in novels such as David Lodge's *Small World*, where Professor Robin Dempsey interacts with Eliza, one of the first computer programs to attempt to simulate conversation. Eliza (the name, indeed, being borrowed from Shaw's character Eliza Doolittle in *Pygmalion*) was devised by Joseph Weizenbaum in the 1960s, with the dialogue options based on interviews between psychiatrists and patients.

Having been instructed in how to use the computer, Dempsey types in HALLO and Eliza replies HALLO, HOW ARE YOU FEELING?

'I'M FEELING TERRIBLE,' Robin replied.
'WHAT DO YOU MEAN BY THAT PRECISELY?'
'I'M FEELING DEPRESSED.'
'WHY DO YOU THINK YOU ARE DEPRESSED?'
'BECAUSE I'M LONELY.'
'DO YOU LIVE WITH YOUR FAMILY?'
'NO.'
'DO YOU HAVE ANY FRIENDS?'
'NOT REALLY.'
'WHY IS THAT?'

And so the chat continues, demonstrating a level of respectful turn-taking, succinct syntax, and persistent interrogation that defies all the conversational practices I described earlier.

Novelists such as Lodge, and Jodi Picoult and Rick Riordan in my Prologue, show us some very different conversations in their writing, and Eliza is out of the Ark compared with present-day human–computer conversations, which are much more colloquial and wide-ranging (Chapter 18). But which robot could—or would ever want to—cope with Haruki Murakami's character in the short story 'Firefly':

> These days I just can't seem to say what I mean . . . I just can't. Every time I try to say something, it misses the point. Either that or I end up saying the opposite of what I mean. The more I try to get it right the more mixed up it gets. Sometimes I can't even remember what I was trying to say in the first place. It's like my body's split in two and one of me is chasing the other me around a big pillar. We're running circles around it. The other me has the right words, but I can never catch her.

Chapter Twelve

THE VOCAL AND THE VISUAL

We all know what 'natural, spontaneous, everyday, domestic, informal conversation' is because we use it every day. It makes up most of our speaking lives. Yet it is a variety that's extremely difficult to describe in a scientific way. For how is it to be recorded so that its spontaneity is not affected? The problem is a familiar one in social studies, where it's known that the presence of an observer influences the behaviour of the people being observed. And in the study of speech, it's immediately obvious: as soon as people see a microphone, and know they're being recorded, they begin to speak in a self-conscious way—with some finding themselves unable to speak fluently at all!

To solve this problem, in the early days of data collection for surveys of usage, researchers would sometimes hide the microphone so that conversations were surreptitiously recorded. Today, such a procedure would raise a raft of ethical issues that were simply not being thought about in the 1960s. But in any case, that way of working didn't achieve the desired result. The settings were typically university laboratories, where colleagues were the subjects—and the kind of conversation recorded, we can readily imagine, was not likely to be representative of the way people talked in less academic settings. Nor was it always possible to hear what the people were saying. If you hide a microphone under a table or behind a curtain, it's not always going to pick up everything that's being said because people move around, turn their heads, push things about, bang the table with their hands, and generally behave in such a way that the recording can be of limited value. Nor was it always easy to distinguish the participants, especially when more than two people were conversing.

How to marry unconscious spontaneity and good recording quality? I adopted a different procedure for my contribution to the *Advanced Conversational English* project. (*Advanced* here simply meant 'normal'— an ironic comment on the way traditional teaching courses used dialogues that were some way removed from everyday conversational practice.) I would ask two or three friends or acquaintances to my house for an evening. In some cases, they knew each other well (two of the couples were married); in others, they hadn't met before, or hadn't seen each other for some time. All were in their 20s or 30s. I would tell them in advance that they were going to be recorded— for a research project into English accents, and as they all had wonderful voices...Nobody refused. Come the evening, when the visitors arrived I would show them into the sitting room, where each had an armchair beside which was a microphone on a stand. When they sat down, the mike was quite close to their mouths, so that the auditory quality of the recording would be excellent. And all the mikes had cables leading to a large tape recorder in the middle of the room. (This was the early 1970s, remember. No wi-fi or smartphones then.)

After a welcome, and an opening drink, the evening began. I explained what they would have to do for the accent project—just count from one to twenty in their normal voices. I turned the tape recorder on, and each person solemnly did as they were asked. Then I turned the recorder off, thanked them very much, and let the evening take its conversational course. At one point, I had to leave the room for an unexpected telephone call. Kept me away for over twenty minutes. My apologies.

Of course, as readers will by now have guessed, the microphones weren't linked to the visible tape recorder at all, but to a different one in the kitchen, and this was the machine that recorded the entire evening of conversation. The speakers didn't bother moving the microphones, which stayed by their sides all evening. There was no reason to; they weren't in their way. So the quality of the recording remained good. And because they had seen the visible tape recorder switched off, the participants all relaxed, and spoke as they normally would in an informal setting. My absence was to avoid unconsciously influencing their conversation.

Later in the evening, I would come clean, tell my visitors what I had done, and explain why. I offered them the option of deleting the recording, bearing in mind that they might have felt something they said was untoward. If they were happy, there would of course be total anonymity, and if their names or other personal details were mentioned in a recording (as in the Gerry/Tony dialogue), these segments would not be used, unless they gave permission for them to stay. Several conversations were recorded in this way, and I was never asked to delete anything. The only obligation I was presented with came from my two football-supporting friends, who made me promise that, whenever we should meet again, it would always—*always*—be my turn to buy the drinks! And so it has proved to be.

The result was the kind of conversation illustrated throughout this book, and it was unlike anything I had ever been able to analyse before. Today, with conversation analysis having developed into a major domain of linguistic enquiry, generating many descriptive studies, the novelty of the findings has worn off somewhat, and several other investigative procedures have been devised. It's also the case, these days, that people are much more used to recording themselves and their friends using smart technology, so that the problem of obtaining good-quality, unselfconscious data has receded. Yet the findings of all this work are still little known outside of the research journals. Hence the present book.

Conversations without words

A further consequence of smart technology is that another weakness of the traditional approach can be overcome: the absence of a visual record. It was of course always possible to bring in a video camera to record a conversation, but this was even more intrusive, and the problems of auditory quality and uncertainty remained. A camera would be set up in a particular place, and pointed in a particular direction; it would record well what it saw, but if people went out of shot or were speaking away from the camera's microphone, the old issues would return. Radio microphones helped—if a project could afford them. Today these difficulties are far less serious, and good-quality video recordings of conversations are now easy to make using unobtrusive mobile cameras. The result has been an increased awareness of the importance of the non-verbal behaviour that is part of face-to-face interaction. I mentioned this in passing in an earlier chapter (pp. 48–9), but the point needs further illustration because of the way 'body language' can influence the progress and outcome of a conversation.

In fact, 'body *language*' isn't a good name to describe what is going on, as these features of behaviour lack the complexity and creativity that we associate with spoken and written language. The technical term, used by linguists, psychologists, and other researchers into human behaviour, is *non-verbal communication—NVC* for short. It emerged as a research field in the 1950s, as part of semiotics, the study of patterned human communication in all its five modes— sound, vision, touch, smell, and taste. For humans, it is vision (*kinesic* behaviour) and touch (*proxemic* behaviour) that are important. Kinesics refers to facial expressions, gestures, and body postures; proxemics to body contact and distance. An NVC perspective has increasingly become a part of conversation analysis in recent years.

Both dimensions can be explicitly acknowledged within a conversation. The English television comedian Eric Morecambe used to tease his co-host Ernie Wise with the catchphrase 'Look at me when

I'm talking to you'. People attach considerable meaning to eye contact, as it signals inclusion. In a multi-party conversation, it's important that a speaker makes occasional eye contact with each person to avoid anyone feeling excluded. 'Occasional' is important: a prolonged gaze takes on its own significance, suggesting that the speaker sees the recipient of the gaze as being especially relevant to the point being made (or perhaps the speaker simply fancies the recipient). It's something that needs to be borne in mind if the topic of the conversation is at all sensitive, to avoid this kind of exchange, talking about office protocol:

> A: it's becoming a real pain / - people are having a cup of coffee in the kitchen and not washing up after them / -
> B: hey / why are you looking at me /
> A: oh I didn't mean you / . . .

To avoid any implication of accusation, the natural strategy is to avoid any eye contact at the critical moment—casting eyes down or turning aside.

But there are times within a conversation when prolonged eye contact is helpful as a selection device if there is more than one listener. If Ann is making a point to Mike and Chris, and she knows that Mike is the one to take the point further, then as she approaches the end of what she wants to say she will look at Mike—in effect, offering him the conversational ball (p. 5). Chris, seeing this, will respect it. Listeners are usually sensitive to this kind of turn-taking cue. Of course if Chris feels the choice is wrong, and wants to speak next, he can intervene and try to override Ann's selection. Two people will then speak at the same time until one concedes.

Listeners use non-verbal cues as well to signal that they want to receive the conversational ball (p. 48). Mike can let Ann know he wants to speak next by moving his body into an anticipatory position—leaning forward, perhaps raising a hand a little, looking directly at her. There is often an accompanying audible intake of breath. There may be a brief vocalization (such as *uh* or *er*) or a more definite utterance-beginning (*I...*, *I think...*, *But...*). These interpolations are not intended to be interruptions; they are simply attention-getting signals. And Ann can respect them or ignore them. If she doesn't want to yield the floor at that point she will show this by *not* looking at Mike—indeed, not looking at any of her listeners. And here too the non-verbal communication can be explicitly acknowledged. Mike might say to Ann later, 'I was trying to catch your eye'.

Distance can also be involved in the dynamic of a conversation, especially if people are free to move while they talk—standing together rather than sitting on chairs. They may move closer together if the topic warrants a greater intimacy. They may even touch each other— the speaker's hand brushing the listener's arm to show extra friendliness, a push of a shoulder in a jokey exchange, a grasp of an arm to convey greater intensity of meaning. Political observers always pay great attention to such things when we see one country leader meeting another on television. However, it should be noted that such behaviours are very much conditioned by social and cultural considerations. Touching would be considered wholly unacceptable in some cultures, even offensive; in others, it is frequent, and its absence would be considered offensive; in others, it is acceptable only between people of the same sex.

Distance is similarly culture-bound. Assuming there is no external constraint (such as people pushed together in a busy pub), how near one person stands to another is an important variable. In some cultures, the comfortable speaking distance may be as much as a metre; in others, much less. Personalities differ too, with one person wanting to move closer to another, while another wants to maintain a greater distance. We give our sense of discomfort expression when we say that someone has 'invaded our personal space'. In multicultural settings, I have often seen a 'conversational dance', when a close-maintainer (let's call her Lisette) talks to a distance-maintainer (let's call him David). Lisette moves close to David to talk, who feels uncomfortable, so he steps back, maintaining a greater distance. Lisette, however, finds this distance uncomfortable, so she comes closer again, forcing David to step back a second time. And so the dance continues.

This is a real story, by the way. I was the David involved, and Lisette was one of my students. I recall circling my office several times while the conversation proceeded. I knew what was going on, but Lisette did not. Throughout the conversation she seemed totally oblivious to the choreography she had initiated.

Acting out the story

There are also instances where the non-verbal communication is topic-driven. An example of this occurs in Recording 1, when Tony is describing the features of a football ground:

> they had . they had it s organized / in such a way / that there was so many entrances all round / – m you know / . arcs / like this / upstairs downstairs /

Like this is totally unclear in an audio recording. Only in a video recording would we be able to see the shapes he was making with his hands to show the situation. Words like *this, that, here*, and *there* are often used in this way. Linguists call them *deictic* (pronounced [dike-tik]) words, from a Greek word meaning 'show'. Their purpose is to show the listener where an action is taking place: *put the book here, the exit is over there, look at that*. We need to see the location in order to understand what the speaker is saying. Personal pronouns are deictic too. Sentences such as *look at him* and *they're nice-looking* need context before they make sense. Of course, in a conversation the meaning may be obvious from what's just been said. But at any time a pronoun might be used to refer to something the speakers see that they suddenly want to talk about, and because it's visually obvious they don't bother saying explicitly what it is.

Children do this a lot when they're talking about what they see in a book. Here's an example from a conversation between a mother and her little girl:

MOTHER: so what's happening in the picture /
GIRL: he's in a bus and she's in a car /
MOTHER: and where do you think they're going /
GIRL: I think they're going on holidays / cos look / you can see it /

I needed to see her book to find out that *he* was a bus driver, *she* was in a taxi, and *it* referred to the beach. This is not very different from the kind of conversation people have when they are talking about what they're seeing—a television picture, a painting in an art gallery, an animal in the zoo.

There's one other kind of non-verbal behaviour that we find in conversation, especially when someone is telling a story. We might call it 'the dramatic moment'. The speaker reaches a critical point, and then pauses to do something—have a drink, light a cigarette, take out a handkerchief, walk over to a window...Listeners (and viewers) are made to wait for the resolution. It's an option often seen in novels and films. John le Carré's character George Smiley has a habit, described in *Tinker Tailor Soldier Spy* (Chapter 6): 'His only fidget was to polish his glasses on the silk lining of his tie.' And later in the story (Chapter 34) we see him using the habit at a crucial point in his conversation with Toby Esterhase about the identity of the 'mole' in London's spy network. George has been giving a detailed analysis of the situation, and then asks the big question:

'Who meets him, Toby? Who has the handling of Polyakov? You? Roy? Bill?'

Taking the fat end of his tie, Smiley turned the silk lining outwards and began polishing his glasses. 'Everyone does,' he said, answering his own question.

This is non-verbal communication as theatre, and indeed it is in the theatrical world that we find the natural world of everyday conversation, visual and vocal, given its full artistic expression.

Dickensian pauses

Charles Dickens was a keen observer of the way visual and vocal effects combine in a conversation. One of his favourite narrative techniques is to describe a character pausing and doing something before carrying on:

> 'What do you think them women does t'other day,' continued Mr. Weller, after a short pause, during which he had significantly struck the side of his nose with his forefinger some half-dozen times. 'What do you think they does, t'other day, Sammy?' (*The Pickwick Papers*, Chapter 22)

> 'There's many men I can't compare with, who never could have loved my little Dot like me, I think!'
>
> He paused, and softly beat the ground a short time with his foot, before resuming. 'I often thought that though I wasn't good enough for her.' (*The Cricket on the Hearth*, Chapter 3)

He often adds an accompanying interpretative comment:

> 'If we mean the same gentleman, as I suppose we do,' Hugh rejoined softly, 'I tell you this—he's as good and quick information about everything as—' here he paused and looked round, as if to make sure that the person in question was not within hearing, 'as Old Nick himself.' (*Barnaby Rudge*, Chapter 53)

> 'But—really, you know, Mr. Stryver—' Mr. Lorry paused, and shook his head at him in the oddest manner, as if he were compelled against his will to add, internally, 'you know there really is so much too much of you!' (*A Tale of Two Cities*, Chapter 18)

Chapter Thirteen

CONVERSATION AS THEATRE

For most people, the main impression of the nature of conversation comes from the way it is written down in books or in scripts. It's a misleading impression, as the conversations we read in novels or plays have been artistically structured, and revised—often many times—before being put on public display. And those we hear on stage and screen are—with just the occasional improvisatory exception—also the product of revision and rehearsal. The unpredictability and interactive randomness of everyday conversation, noted in earlier chapters, is missing. Even in the most improvised of play conversations, as in Mike Leigh's films, there is an underlying storyline which the characters need to follow. As the director put it, in a 2011 interview reported in ActorHub:

> What I shoot is quite structured. Though the dialogue may at times be improvised, the intentions are all planned and very precise.

This is not to say that the conversations in a play are totally identical each time they are performed: actors often say that 'no two performances are the same', and when the opportunity to compare arises, it is indeed the case that a multiplicity of variations in tone of voice, intonation, and other prosodic features come to light, as well as alterations in timing, as actors interpret and develop their roles. The variations are even more noticeable when different productions of the same play are compared—something that is easy to do these days, with productions available on video or the Internet. A famous sentence, such as Hamlet's *to be or not to be*, has received countless variations. Samuel West, in an interview for BBC Online (23 September 2010) illustrated several performance options: *to be* (with a level tone) followed by a one-beat pause and then a breathy falling tone on *not to be*; *to be* (with a rising tone) followed by pauses before and after *or*, and then a resonant *not to be*; and so on. And there was a famous occasion in 2016 at the Royal Shakespeare Company, celebrating the 400th anniversary of Shakespeare's death, when some of the country's best-known actors participated in a skit giving their personal renditions of the line, concluding with the arrival of Prince Charles (it can be seen online: see references, p. 198). Disagreement focused on which word in the line was to receive the peak of prominence, with each actor choosing a different word (HRH chose *question*). But the range of variations heard in performance are nonetheless seriously constrained by overriding considerations to do with the actor's (and director's) interpretation of the character, the theme, and the nature of soliloquy. They little resemble the fluctuations of everyday conversation noted in earlier chapters.

Rehearsed conversations

Are daily informal conversations ever rehearsed? In preparing this book, I asked several people if they ever carried on anticipatory conversations in their head. All said they did. The typical case is when an awkward or unwanted situation is looming, and they think up possible initiatives, directions, and responses. The reality is likely to be very different, of course, but people admit to feeling more comfortable if they have thought through a possible scenario in advance— or at least the opening moves. In a more formal situation, such as an interview, responses to expected questions may be rehearsed in some detail—and even given oral expression, either alone or in front of a sympathetic listener.

We encounter a different kind of rehearsal when we talk to someone whose job it is to engage in conversation with us, such as a call-centre operative. When the employee is a commercial salesperson, and the conversation is face-to-face, the 'patter' has a distinctively unoriginal character. Training will have introduced the employee (or the robot, these days) to a schedule of greetings, questions, and points of information. Quite specific points of interaction will have been addressed, such as how to introduce oneself (*Hello. My name is Trevor. How may I help?*) or (in the case of 'cold calls') how the recipient is to be addressed (*Good morning, David. How are you today?*). If the encounter is taking place over a phone, an announcement may be made that the conversation will be recorded 'for training purposes'.

I was actually once involved myself in a training process. A ferry company asked me to listen to its announcements and call-in conversations, and advise on how they might be improved, as it was receiving complaints from customers about the quality of their experience. It wasn't difficult to see why. The commonest problem was that the operatives were speaking too quickly for the customer to take in what was being said, as evidenced by repeated requests to 'please say that again'. It's an easy trap to fall into: there's a natural tendency to speed up when you find yourself explaining the same point over and over to different customers. And if the speaker has a regional accent that is unfamiliar to the listener, this tends to broaden when speed increases, producing a greater level of unintelligibility. Often, accent is unfairly blamed for the resulting lack of comprehension when it's actually the underlying speech rate that is the cause of the problem. This is particularly noticeable when companies in a country where stress-timed rhythm ('tum-te-tum-te-tum') is the norm (such as Britain) outsource their call-centres to a part of the world where syllable-timed rhythm ('rat-a-tat-a-tat') is the norm (such as India).

I've tried to obtain information about the retraining process that companies employ, but they're reluctant to cooperate. I suppose it's only natural that they wouldn't wish their unsatisfactory performance to be monitored by outsiders, and I imagine, if ever linguistic consultants *were* allowed inside, it would involve them signing a non-disclosure agreement. But there are certainly benefits from introducing a pragmatic perspective into company conversational practice, because even quite basic insights are regularly ignored. An example from my own experience is the *Good morning, David* I referred to above. This was a cold call from someone with an American accent, who had researched my name, and obviously been trained to get on first-name terms from the outset. Now while first-naming on first encounter is culturally common in the USA, the practice is 'not British', and it easily antagonizes. I put the phone down without listening further. And then, to check that this wasn't just me, I asked several people from the UK what they would feel if addressed in this way. The response was universally negative. 'I might just put the phone down,' said one, 'which would stop me getting irritated.' (In pragmatic terms, the intention behind the caller's utterance—the *illocutionary force*—had an undesired *perlocutionary effect* on the recipient.)

A further scenario of rehearsed informality occurs in chat shows, such as on radio, TV, or on stage—as in the 'conversation with an author' that is common in literary festivals. I've often been in a green room at a litfest and heard the author and the interviewer prepare for their one-hour event. There is agreement about what is to be talked about—and what is not to be talked about—and the order in which the topics will be addressed. The resulting conversation sounds really spontaneous, but in fact there is little topical unpredictability—though I do know some authors who take a delight in wrong-footing their interviewer by introducing an unexpected topic into the conversation or vice versa. They are the occasions that people especially enjoy, with famous chat show disasters now remembered for ever thanks to YouTube.

This is conversation for the benefit of third parties—in this case a listening or viewing audience—in which the participants are very conscious of how they are presenting themselves. It is talk as deliberate theatre. And it may involve a fourth party, in the form of a programme producer, who can instruct the presenter through headphones to take the conversation in a particular direction. Having been in the control room during a political television programme, I was surprised at the number of comments or suggestions being fed to the presenter in the course of the interview. And as a consultant to a TV chat show on English usage in 2006, *Never Mind the Full Stops*, I was in the control room to see an episode in which host Julian Fellowes quizzed and prompted the two teams—Jessica Fellowes and Gyles Brandreth vs Sue Carroll and Roger McGough—and found myself asked several times by the producer for suggestions that were then fed through to Julian. The same thing can happen visually on radio, where in a studio there can be a monitor screen on which the producer sends points to the presenter—or, in the case of a phone-in programme, information about the next caller. Viewers don't usually notice what is happening, as presenters assimilate the points and take the conversation in a fresh direction without any noticeable disjointedness.

I see everyday face-to-face conversation and play scripts as representing two ends of a spectrum. Situations in which there is a degree of preparation or rehearsal result in conversations that, although remaining informal, are more structured than would be found elsewhere. And the conversations found in novels, plays, and other literary genres display a similar diversity.

Literary conversations

Part of Shakespeare's skill as a dramatist was his ability to present the range of Elizabethan English conversation in all its stylistic diversity, from maximally formal to maximally informal. To take just one play, *Romeo and Juliet*. At one extreme, we have the first encounter between the two lovers (1.5.93), where the conversation is not only in verse but takes the form of a sonnet in which each person speaks symmetrically:

ROMEO: If I profane with my unworthiest hand
　　This holy shrine, the gentle sin is this.
　　My lips, two blushing pilgrims, ready stand
　　To smooth that rough touch with a tender kiss.
JULIET: Good pilgrim, you do wrong your hand too much,
　　Which mannerly devotion shows in this.
　　For saints have hands that pilgrims' hands do touch,
　　And palm to palm is holy palmers' kiss.
ROMEO: Have not saints lips, and holy palmers too?
JULIET: Ay, pilgrim, lips that they must use in prayer.
ROMEO: O, then, dear saint, let lips do what hands do!
They pray: grant thou, lest faith turn to despair.
JULIET: Saints do not move, though grant for prayers' sake.
ROMEO: Then move not while my prayer's effect I take.

At the other extreme, we have colloquial dialogue, as in this fast-moving piece of banter between Romeo and Mercutio (2.4.49):

ROMEO: Pardon, good Mercutio. My business was great, and in such
　　a case as mine a man may strain courtesy.
MERCUTIO: That's as much as to say, such a case as yours con-
　　strains a man to bow in the hams [legs].
ROMEO: Meaning, to curtsy.
MERCUTIO: Thou hast most kindly hit it.
ROMEO: A most courteous exposition.
MERCUTIO: Nay, I am the very pink of courtesy.
ROMEO: Pink for flower.
MERCUTIO: Right.
ROMEO: Why, then is my pump [shoe] well-flowered.

A little later in the scene (2.4.159), we have colloquial monologue, as the Nurse cautions Romeo, with a copious use of adverbial pointers and comment clauses (p. 73):

Pray you, sir, a word; and, as I told you, my young lady bid me inquire you out. What she bid me say, I will keep to myself. But first let me tell ye, if ye should lead her in a fool's paradise, as they say, it were a very gross kind of behaviour, <u>as they say</u>. For the gentlewoman is young; and therefore if you should deal double with her, <u>truly</u> it were an ill thing to be offered to any gentlewoman, and very weak dealing.

The stylistic function of the underlined items is clear if we rewrite the passage omitting them:

Sir, a word; and, my young lady bid me inquire you out. What she bid me say, I will keep to myself. But if ye should lead her in a fool's paradise, it were a very gross kind of behaviour. For the gentlewoman is young; and therefore if you should deal double with her, it were an ill thing to be offered to any gentlewoman, and very weak dealing.

The speech now sounds very business-like, quite out of character.

Comment clauses, linking adverbs, attention-getting words, and so on can be seen as soon as writers began to include conversation in their work. The oldest recorded English conversation (p. 19) contains them. Here is the master addressing the monk in Ælfric's *Colloquy*:

Eala, munuc, þe me tospycst, efne, ic hæbbe afandod þe habban gode geferan.

Eala is a word used to focus attention, translatable as 'so', 'well', 'I say', or the like. *Efne* here is an emphasizer, translatable as 'lo', 'truly', 'indeed'. The sentence as a whole might thus be translated as follows:

So, monk, you who have spoken to me, indeed, I have shown that you have good companions.

Chaucer repeatedly uses colloquial interpolations, as in this extract from *The Reeve's Tale* (lines 4023ff. of *The Canterbury Tales*):

Aleyn spak first: 'Al hayl, Symond, <u>y-fayth</u>!
 [Aleyn spoke first: 'All hail, Symond, in faith!]
Hou fares thy faire doghter and thy wyf?'
 [How fares thy fair daughter and thy wife?]
'Aleyn, welcome,' quod Symkyn, <u>'by my lyf</u>!
 ['Aleyn, welcome,' said Symkyn, 'by my life!]

And John also, <u>how now</u>, what do ye heer?'
 [And John also, how now, what do you here?']
'Symond,' quod John, '<u>by God</u>, nede has na peer.
 ['Symond,' said John, 'by God, need has no equal.]
Hym boes serve hymself that has na swayn,
 [He must serve himself who has no servant,]
Or elles he is a fool, <u>as clerkes sayn</u>.'
 [Or else he is a fool, as clerks say.']

The four very frequent modern comment clauses all have a long history. *You see* and *you know* are both recorded from the fourteenth century. *I mean* is used by Gonzalo in *The Tempest* (2.1.104):

Is not, sir, my doublet as fresh as the first day
I wore it? I mean, in a sort.

Mind you is the most recent to arrive, recorded only in the eighteenth century. The parenthetic function is usually explicitly shown by punctuation—even, in early typesetting, by round brackets, as in this extract from the First Folio text of *Cymbeline* (5.4.93):

No more, you petty Spirits of Region low,
Offend our hearing: hush. How dare you Ghostes
Accuse the Thunderer, whose Bolt (you know)
Sky-planted, batters all rebelling Coasts.

This is Jupiter addressing the mother and brothers of Posthumus. Even the gods deign to be conversational sometimes, especially when they're cross.

Literature thus readily provides us with multiple examples of the diverse ways in which conversations work, illustrating the spectrum of options between the extremes of everyday face-to-face interaction and play dialogue. But within this spectrum there is a domain that adds a further dimension to our understanding of the nature of conversation, already hinted at by my references to BBC Online and YouTube in the earlier part of this chapter: the Internet.

Always a conversation

Sometimes the notion of conversation is enormously broadened to take in the whole world of reading and writing. Laurence Sterne, for example, in *The Life and Opinions of Tristram Shandy* (1760, Book 2, Chapter 11), imagines himself to be taking part in a conversation with his readers:

> Writing, when properly managed, (as you may be sure I think mine is) is but a different name for conversation.

And a modern view: Neil Gaiman, in *The View from the Cheap Seats* (2016):

> Literature does not occur in a vacuum. It cannot be a monologue. It has to be a conversation, and new people, new readers, need to be brought into the conversation too.

In a complementary way, René Descartes in his *Discourse on Method* (translation by F. E. Sutcliffe, 1637, Book 1) describes reading as a conversation with writers:

> To read good books is like holding a conversation with the most eminent minds of past centuries and, moreover, a studied conversation in which these authors reveal to us only the best of their thoughts.

Bangambiki Habyarimana, in *Pearls of Eternity* (2016), extends the theme to its inevitable conclusion:

> A writer is never alone: he is always in conversation with himself.

Spoken monologues too may be conceived as conversations. I know several academic lecturers (including me) who see their lectures in this way. Some allow interventions throughout; others insist on a question-and-answer period at the end. And an online not-for-profit periodical for academic research and analysis, launched in Australia in 2011, and now with editions in several countries, is called simply: *The Conversation.*

Chapter Fourteen

ONLINE 'CONVERSATIONS'

Conversations in novels differ from those recorded in plays. Plays are written to be read aloud. In novels, the conversations are written to be read in silence, and if we hear them read aloud (as in an audio book), the reader faithfully reproduces the narrative conventions in the text, such as the use of 'say' verbs and associated adverbials: *he said angrily, she declared in a frosty tone*. These are not usually found in play scripts, unless the author feels the need to point an emotion or clarify the direction of a speech: *MARLON* (*bitterly*), *MARLON* (*to Trevor*). How do person-to-person Internet exchanges, such as in emails, WhatsApp, instant messaging, and social media forums, compare to these two genres from a conversational point of view?

They are called conversations, as they display the crucial property of turn-taking, and the identity of the participants is explicitly recognized by the software; but their linguistic character is unique. To begin with, they don't use the 'say' convention of novels or the parenthetic convention of plays. Instead, if the sender wants to draw attention to an attitude, emoticons and emojis are available:

'I'm not going,' he said angrily.
MARLON (*angrily*): I'm not going.
I'm not going. :((

These symbols are among the most distinctive orthographic features of Internet exchanges, used both at the end of a sentence, and (more frequently) as a replacement for a sentence. However, they can only partly translate what would be expressed through language—which is perhaps why they have had only a limited presence in e-messages—as they are inherently ambiguous. What is the meaning of a 'smiling' emoticon? Pleasure? Delight? A joke? Sarcasm? An ironic remark? A pseudo-friendly welcome ('Come in, Mr Bond...')? Everything depends on the context. In this respect, the more explicit descriptions in novels have no equal, as in Ian Fleming's *Goldfinger* (1959), where Du Pont smiles 'wetly', and Goldfinger smiles 'politely' at Bond, and later (Chapter 11) 'thinly':

> Goldfinger turned to Bond. He said conversationally, 'This is my handy man.' He smiled thinly. 'That is something of a joke. Oddjob, show Mr Bond your hands.' He smiled again at Bond. 'I call him Oddjob because that describes his functions on my staff.'

No emoticon or emoji captures nuances of this kind.

The contrast with everyday face-to-face conversations as described in this book can be clearly seen in this extract from a WhatsApp exchange—here shown without the colour contrasts, screen layout, and other organizational features, and with names added. It is very similar in topic variation and level of informality to the kind of conversations illustrated earlier in this book; but several important features are not to be seen, and there are some additional features relating specifically to the graphic medium, notably the use of non-standard spelling, punctuation, and capitalization.

> EVE: how did you get on at the meeting?
> JILL: it went well
> EVE: what time did it finish?
> JILL: about an hour ago
> JILL: it lasted longer than I was expecting
> EVE: you still managed to get the early evening train though
> JILL: but it was worth it
> JILL: Mike spent a lot of time listening to our ideas and he said he'd read our stuff asap :))

EVE: brilllll!

JILL: i was really worried in case the early items on the agenda would take up too much time, but in the end it was ok – & it turned out that theyd allowd a bit of time for extra char anyway

JILL: *chat

EVE: char sounds good actually – you'll probably want some when you get in

EVE: or maybe some thing stronger

JILL: :)))

EVE: i was actually expecting we'd have to find another date to get things finished off, and that wouldve been really difficult cos I'm away all next month

What is missing? There is no simultaneous feedback, for a start (Chapter 5), nor could there be, given the nature of the medium. There is successive feedback, of course, but while one person is typing, the other can provide no reaction. That is why, in longer texts (such as emails), it's important to read through the message before pressing 'send'. In everyday conversation, an ambiguous or disturbing remark can be self-corrected immediately, when listeners provide this feedback to speakers. In Internet exchanges, this is not an option, so there will be a delay before the impact of any unintended remark will manifest itself. Nor could there be any interruptions (Chapter 6). Even in video interactions, such as Skype, the phenomenon of lag—the slight time delay between the moment of speaking and the moment of hearing—makes natural simultaneous feedback unwieldy, and users, sensing this, tend to avoid it.

Less obviously, comment clauses are missing too (Chapter 8). In any corpus of Internet exchanges, expressions such as *you know, you see, I mean*, and *mind you* are conspicuous by their absence. Even *be/go* + *like*—a characteristic of young people's narratives typically used when quoting a remark (*I was, like, Are you serious?*; *Jim goes, like, Wow*)—is unusual. The economy of the exchanges must be partly the reason. With short sentences containing self-evident content, there is little motivation to introduce the breathing points or signposts

that speakers use to add clarification or to maintain the flow of a
longer narrative. But colloquial comment clauses of this kind are
unusual even in messages where length is greater, such as a blog post
or a lengthy email. Why is this?

It may be a function of the lack of prosody. In speech, an expression such as *you know* has a variety of intonation, loudness, and tempo
patterns depending on where in the sentence it occurs and the meaning to be conveyed. Writing struggles to manifest these distinctions.
A spelling such as *y'know* captures a speeding up, but a slowing down
has no standard convention (despite occasional experiments with
such forms as *knooow* and *knoooow*), and *you know!*, *you know?*, *you
know?!*, and suchlike give no clear indication of how they should be
said and interpreted. Alternatively, it may be that comment clauses
are not needed because their meanings are better expressed through
emoticons and emojis—for example, a winking face to capture the 'I
know something' usage:

> Mike and his, you know, friend were in the bar
> Mike and his ;-) friend were in the bar
> *or*
> Mike and his friend were in the bar ;-)

But at least these examples are like offline conversations in two crucial respects: they are between two people who know each other and
who are talking to each other at the same point in time. Most online
chats aren't like that.

'Conversations'

The Internet strains our traditional understanding of conversation
in several ways, to the extent that it's questionable whether the interaction can legitimately be called by that name. To begin with, an online
chat can continue indefinitely. The phenomenon isn't entirely new,
for people do say such things as 'We must continue this conversation

another time' and 'Mark and I have been having this conversation for several years', but the crucial point is that in these situations the participants stay the same, aware of their shared background. What makes Internet conversations different is the number of people who contribute to them and the nature of their relationship over the extended period of time. There can be any number, and in most contexts they're unlikely to know each other outside of their online interaction, so there's no shared background other than what they recall from their forum history. I'm reminded again of Sarah Orne Jewitt's observation in my Prologue: 'Conversation's got to have some root in the past, or else you've got to explain every remark you make, an' it wears a person out.' And if the participants cloak their identity under a nickname, and avoid giving personal details, there's no way we can know anything about their age, gender, status, interests, cultural background, and so on. It's difficult to imagine anything less like everyday face-to-face conversation.

The stylistic character of online conversation changes as a consequence. One effect of anonymity has been well discussed in the media: the increase in abuse, intolerance, and extreme views. Less noticed has been the greater directness that characterizes online exchanges. A well-studied pragmatic feature of everyday face-to-face conversation is the way speakers avoid imposing an obligation on their listeners. Studies of requests, for example, have shown how direct commands are replaced by questions using pronoun shifts that spread the responsibility (*Open the window* becomes *Would you mind if we opened the window?*) or move to an even more indirect expression (*It's really hot in here, don't you think?*). Direct *yes/no* questions can also be problematic because they force respondents to choose when they might prefer not to have to. The search for an escape route is evidenced when we hear such responses as *That might not be such a good idea, I wonder what the others think?*, and *It might be better to wait*. Because any of us can be placed in such an uncomfortable position, we are aware of the ever-present danger lurking inside a *yes/no* question, and we avoid putting our listeners into the position of having to say *no*. There are hardly any instances of *no* responses in all my recordings, and when they do occur they are *no*'s of agreement with a statement:

A: I didn't really enjoy the flames very much /
B: no /

Online, the opposite is the case. Direct questions and monosyllabic responses are common, even though sometimes stylistically softened by emoticons and emojis.

Many Internet 'conversations' are also unusual in that there may be interference from an outside party—a 'big brother' monitor or editor, whose role is to sanitize words or views that are unpalatable to the website owners. Swear words are the usual target, but offensive language of any kind can be removed or replaced. An overview of a series of forum exchanges can thus at times take on a very odd appearance, with a response remaining visible although the original stimulus has disappeared. Or an utterance becomes ungrammatical because the swear word has been removed while leaving the rest of the sentence intact. Such phenomena are virtually impossible to explore scientifically, for all this activity takes place 'behind the scenes'. An editor/monitor who was also a linguist could provide some interesting answers here—if ever allowed to do so.

The extended time-frame of Internet conversations raises a further issue. It's perfectly possible for someone to add to a dialogue at any point in the future (assuming the website stays live). Here's an example, from a blog post I wrote in July 2011. A correspondent had written to ask if I knew of any recorded examples of people speaking with their mouth full. He was thinking of food, but I pulled together a number of other situations, such as someone speaking with a mouth filled with such things as a pin, a pen, or a cigarette, and found a couple of examples where novelists had reported the behaviour in a conversation, as in Charles Dickens' *Nicholas Nickleby* (Chapter 5):

'This is the way we inculcate strength of mind, Mr Nickleby,' said the schoolmaster, turning to Nicholas, and speaking with his mouth very full of beef and toast.

I wasn't able to find any instances of novelists trying to represent the segmental phonetics of mouth-filled speech, though, so I asked my readers to let me know of any. And they did. The next day I was sent a quotation from a Harry Potter novel (*The Order of the Phoenix*), where Ron Weasley asks *Ow kunnit nofe skusin danger ifzat?* through a mouthful of roast potatoes ('How can it know the school's in danger if it's a hat?'). And over the next couple of months, into September, the examples continued to come in, and each time I acknowledged with a word of thanks. One of the contributors gave his name as *Stan*. Then there was a break of six years—but Stan evidently never forgot the post, for in June 2017 he sent me another example, and then more into the middle of 2018. I could thus say, with some truth, that I've been having a 'conversation' with Stan for over a year—or over several years, if we take 2011 as the starting point.

These conversations—if they can be labelled such—have some very strange properties. Contributors may never see or respond to later postings. In the extreme case, they may have died in the interim—as actually happened during the timeline of one of my blogs. And because the time-frame is so extended, there may be a lack of semantic coherence: later contributors may talk about topics unrelated to those introduced by the initiator, or may refer to events that were simply not known when the blog began—for example, referring in 2019 to Brexit in a political forum that began in 2004. It no longer makes sense to talk about a conversation 'as a whole', in these cases, for in principle it has no ending. Nor can we easily answer the question 'What was the conversation about?', for it would be anachronistic to say 'Brexit' about a political chat that began in 2004. We need a new term to describe this lack of temporal and semantic coherence: I call them *panchronic* conversations.

Generalizations about online linguistic conversations are dangerous because the medium changes so quickly. For example, in 2006, when Twitter began, the conversation was initiated by a prompt: 'What are you doing?' The result was a lot of present tense narrative and first person pronouns. Then in November 2009 Twitter changed its prompt to 'What's happening?' That immediately led to tweets showing tense variation and third person pronouns, as people began to talk about events that had just happened or were about to happen. A study on the language of Twitter, begun in 2008, would think of itself as being on the cutting edge of linguistic research. Two years later, it would seem to have been more an exercise in historical linguistics. I'll discuss ongoing online change further in Chapter 18.

Online help

The lack of simultaneous feedback in online conversations was highlighted in a *Guardian Online* report about helplines such as the Samaritans and Childline (19 November 2018, by Poppy Noor: 'Can helplines survive our growing fear of the phone call?'). For children, texts and emails now far exceed phone calls, and there's a growing reluctance to use smartphones for oral communication. Childline reported that contacts increased by 44% after it brought in online counselling in 2009, and 73% of its counselling sessions took place online in 2017.

The Samaritans commissioned research into the effectiveness of their email line:

> It concluded that email support was seen as meaningful and positive for most people, but there were some teething troubles. Volunteers talked about finding it hard to convey empathy in writing, or to match the verbal cues that were readily available on the phone. 'I wish there was some way [we could convey] "Uh-huh" or "Mmm" or "Wow" or whatever—just a kind of "Tell me more" kind of noise,' said one.

The lack of prosodic cues was also emphasized in relation to building rapport. One helpline supervisor commented:

> We don't have our voice on webchat. If you listen to mine, I come from Northern Ireland and it's a soft voice. That's helpful for children, but online I can't bring in warmth, tone, pace, anything like that.

Chapter Fifteen

CULTURAL CONVERSATIONS

The anonymity of the Internet makes national and cultural identities opaque. In a chat room there's little chance of identifying the different parts of the world that the participants are from, or their cultural background, unless they say something explicitly. By contrast, in face-to-face conversation, cultural differences are likely to be self-evident or easily establishable, and they manifest themselves in every facet of discourse.

Turn-taking can be affected, especially if the conversation takes place in a culture which has an established sense of hierarchy. In such cases, we find such factors as age, gender, social class, status, and seniority governing the way in which the conversation proceeds, and participants from a different culture may have trouble identifying the different roles. I found myself in just such a situation in Japan when I visited a bookshop for a talk and a book-signing. After the event I was invited into a side room for tea, where I found myself in the company of the sales assistant who had been looking after me, the head of the department in which my books were located, the bookstore manager, and the bookstore owner. After an initial greeting, in English, we sat there in silence as we drank our tea.

I began to feel uncomfortable, and broke the silence by asking the sales assistant how many books of mine we had sold that day. He looked embarrassed, and bowed to his departmental head, who made an observation about how well sales were going in his department at the moment, and bowed to the manager, who agreed that they were doing very well, and bowed to the owner, who made a nice little speech about how he was very proud to welcome me to his store, where sales were actually exceeding those in other bookstores around the city. He ended by asking the sales assistant how many of my books had been sold that day, and the assistant then supplied me with the details.

Apart from learning the conversational hierarchy, there were other cultural features that I eventually learned to respect—such as the important role of silence. In the anthology *Discover Japan* (1975), one of the commentators on Japanese culture, Don Kenny, describes its significance:

> The Japanese have the wonderful ability to enjoy the company of friends in silence as well as sound. In fact, they sometimes seem to be able to communicate far richer meaning with a pause than with a word. . . . It is equally necessary to learn the rhythms and pauses of the culture in order to achieve the proper timing to contribute to the calm surface effect. This timing, or utilization of the effective pause, is called *ma*.

I wonder if this was the sort of culture Scottish novelist James Robertson had in mind when he had his narrator observe the conversation between Mike and Jean in *And the Land Lay Still*:

> He watches her shaping the words in her head before she lets them out. There is something hugely civilised about allowing long pauses in a conversation. Very few people can stand that kind of silence.

Very few British people, yes. But clearly not always for those elsewhere. And if Dr Johnson is to be believed, there are other cultures where silence is even more problematic. In the 'festival of wit' entitled *A Chaplet of Comus* (1811), this anecdote is reported:

> An eminent foreigner, when he was shewn the British Museum, was very troublesome with many absurd enquiries. 'Now there, sir, (said Johnson,) is the difference between an Englishman and a Frenchman. A Frenchman must always be talking whether he

knows any thing of the matter or not; an Englishman is contented to say nothing when he has nothing to say.'

Cultural style

Silence is one of a large number of cultural variables that make or break a conversation when people from different backgrounds talk to each other. In their handbook *World Business Cultures* (2006), Barry Tomalin and Mike Nicks explore the many factors that facilitate or impede international communication. Their focus is on what happens in the world of business, but many of their points are just as applicable to conversation in general, and to the personalities involved. For example, in Chapter 3 they present six contrasts in conversational style:

DIRECT: I say what I mean. Truth matters.
INDIRECT: I adapt what I say to the situation. Avoiding confrontation matters.

PRECISION: I explain things in detail. Avoidance of misunderstanding is crucial.
SUGGESTION: I infer what I want. I make suggestions. You have to read between the lines.

WHAT/WHY: I say what I want, then, if necessary, I explain why.
WHY/WHAT: You cannot possibly understand what I want unless I explain first *why* I want it. Context and background are all important.

FORMAL: I like respect when you talk to me. Use surnames, titles, and avoid too much colloquial language.
INFORMAL: I like informality, first names, friendly language. I think people who are formal may not want to know me.

NEUTRAL: I keep my feelings to myself. I don't smile too much. I prefer not to touch or be touched.
EMOTIONAL: I believe showing emotion is part of communication. I like to express my feelings.

INTERRUPT: I speak fast. I interrupt people. I am tolerant of inter-
     ruptions.
WAIT YOUR TURN: I use a slow and measured speed. I wait my turn
     to speak. I also dislike being interrupted.

Each one of these can be characteristic of a culture as well as of an
individual. And they are the sorts of issues that often come to light
in fiction. In the opening chapter of Stieg Larsson's *The Girl Who
Played with Fire,* mathematics enthusiast Lisbeth Salander finds herself in the company of 16-year-old George Bland (English translation, 2009):

> Salander found his company surprisingly relaxing. The situation
> was unusual. She hardly ever began conversations with strangers
> just to talk. It was not a matter of shyness. For her, a conversa-
> tion had a straightforward function. *How do I get to the phar-
> macy?*, or *How much does the hotel room cost?* Conversation also
> had a professional function. When she worked as a researcher
> for Dragan Armansky at Milton Security she had never minded
> having a long conversation if it was to ferret out facts. On the
> other hand, she disliked personal discussions, which always led
> to snooping around in areas she considered private. *How old are
> you? Guess. Do you like Britney Spears? Who? What do you think
> of Carl Larsson's paintings?* I've never given them a thought. *Are
> you a lesbian?* Piss off.

Lisbeth wouldn't find it comfortable having a business meeting in
countries like Brazil or Japan, therefore, where the norm is to
engage in small talk or unrelated chat for some time before entering
into the agenda. The contrast in cultural expectations can be a
source of disquiet: negotiators with an Anglo-Saxon temperament
want to 'get to the point' as soon as possible, and can be disturbed
when a meeting seems to be taking ages to get down to business.
Conversely, those who see preliminary chat as an essential part of a
process of 'getting to know you' can find a quick-fire agenda equally
disturbing.

Topic choice

Topic choice has two sides: what to talk about and what not to talk about, and these are always culture-sensitive. The issues go well beyond the 'famous five' topics: politics, money (especially personal income), religion, race, and sex. Some examples:

- In a conversation where some of the people are meeting for the first time, or don't know each other well, a common ice-breaking question is to enquire about each other's family. *Do you have children?*, *How old are they?*, *What do they do?* These would be embarrassing or even painful questions in China, which introduced a one-child policy in 1979 to limit population growth.

- In the UK, if John arrives at Mike's house, and his wife is not there, it is perfectly proper to ask how she is; but this would be considered a hugely improper question in the Muslim world.

- Enquiring about what one's parents or grandparents did in the war may be well received in the UK and Russia, but not usually in Germany or Japan. The contrast was a source of humour (in the UK, at any rate) in the TV sitcom *Fawlty Towers* (Episode 6), when Basil Fawlty (aka John Cleese) has a group of German guests in his hotel, and goes about telling people 'Don't mention the war'.

Then there is the question of what one is expected to talk about in the opening of a conversation. In many English-speaking countries, the weather is the safest option, as Dr Johnson averred (p. x). Most places are happy to talk about common problems, such as finding a place to park, or the pain of getting through airport security. Most places welcome a chat about the local food and drink. Most homeowners are pleased to receive admiration about their house or furnishings. But expectations do vary. Asking what one does for a living, with the answer followed up by further questions or comments, is perfectly normal in, say, Britain or the USA, but is an uncomfortable topic in several European countries, such as Italy and Germany.

Americans are happy to be asked about the colleges they went to and the societies they belonged to; British people would find it distinctly unusual to be asked, upon first meeting, about their school or university. Sport does quite well cross-culturally as a conversation opener—as long as there's been no local trauma (such as a recent football defeat). But some topics have both safe and dangerous areas. It is safe, for example, to discuss the cost of property in a locality, or car prices, but not to enquire about how much someone paid for their house or car.

If we're unused to having conversations with people from other cultures, the introduction of an unexpected topic can be quite a shock. Having had many such conversations with students and colleagues from all over the world, I was nonetheless taken aback when a Middle Eastern visitor to my home, having admired a pair of curtains in the living room, commented that they must be very expensive and asked us how much they cost. It was no more than a phatic question, but it left us uncertain about how to reply. Enquiring about it later, I was assured that in some countries it was considered polite to enquire about the cost of furnishings. But old cultural habits die hard; and when I found myself visiting one of those countries some time later, I was never able to bring myself to do so. And in the absence of my question, I recall that in one home the host made up for my pragmatic inadequacy by telling me anyway!

Cultural clashes illustrate one of the things that can go wrong in a conversation. At least in all these instances the speakers have the potential ability to put things right. That has been the assumption behind all the chapters in this book. But what happens when this ability isn't there?

A case of cultural misunderstanding

During a visit to a film festival in a small town in the Czech Republic, I had a conversation with two local people, both fluent in English, which went something like this. We were talking about coincidences, and P was telling me about Q, who had just got a job in P's office:

> P: Me and Q both live in Z street. And what's even more of a coincidence is that he lives in 355 and I live in 356.
>
> ME [*jocularly*]: So you can wave to each other, then!
>
> P [*puzzled*]: No.
>
> ME [*confused, thinking that they've perhaps had an argument*]: I mean, you could keep an eye on each other's house, if one of you was away.
>
> P [*even more puzzled*]: Not very easily. I can't see his house from where I live. It's the other end of the street.
>
> ME: But I thought you were neighbours.
>
> P: Not really.
>
> ME: Ah.

I didn't know what to say next, and we moved on to some other subject.

The next day I made enquiries, and discovered what had gone wrong. It transpired that the town's system of house numbering operated on a totally different basis to what I was used to in the UK. In Britain, houses are numbered sequentially in a street, usually with odd numbers down one side and even numbers down the other. So 355 and 356 would probably be opposite each other—or maybe even next to each other (for some streets have linear numbering). But in this town, the houses were numbered using a 'conscription numbering' system that dates back to the eighteenth century on the basis of when they were built and registered. House number 356 was built (or registered) immediately after house number 355. So it was not necessarily the case that 355 and 356 would be opposite or adjacent to each other. That is why P thought it such a coincidence. (An additional 'orientation' numbering system helps the delivery people!)

Chapter Sixteen

BREAKING THE RULES

In the 1970s, philosopher H. P. Grice introduced a characterization of conversation which has become one of the best-known perspectives for research into the pragmatics of spoken discourse. He proposed four 'maxims of conversation' that underlie the efficient cooperative use of language.

Maxim of quality
Try to make your contribution one that is true, specifically:
    Do not say what you believe to be false.
    Do not say that for which you lack adequate evidence.

Maxim of quantity
Make your contribution as informative as is required for the current purposes of the exchange.
Do not make your contribution more informative than is required.

Maxim of manner
Be perspicuous, and specifically:
    Avoid obscurity.
    Avoid ambiguity.
    Be brief.
    Be orderly.

Maxim of relevance
Make your contributions relevant.

We don't always behave exactly according to these principles in a conversation, of course; but people do seem to recognize their role as a perspective within which actual utterances can be judged.

We can challenge people who make false claims; tell them (politely or rudely) to shut up if they talk too much; call them back if they move away from the point; and ask for clarification if they are obscure.

I should add here that the kind of domestic conversation I've been analysing in this book doesn't fit neatly into these categories. When the 'purpose of the exchange' is so vague as 'to have an enjoyable time', then it's impossible to say anything sensible about the maxim of quantity, and there are several points where it's very difficult to define what the conversation is about, so that the notion of relevance also becomes fuzzy. In an intellectual conversation, evidence to support a point is foregrounded, but in domestic settings people often make statements for which there's no evidence at all, and listeners don't seem to mind. Similarly, the manner maxim is frequently flouted: people can be obscure, ambiguous, verbose, and erratic, yet they're allowed to proceed without being challenged. There is a great deal more tolerance in domestic conversation than these maxims suggest.

When Grice thought up the maxims, he hadn't anticipated the Internet, which presents a challenge to all of them. The quality maxim is ignored when people send messages deliberately intended to cause irritation or discord (*trolling*). Electronic junk mail (*spam*) doesn't respect the quantity maxim. It's a common experience to see the recommendations of the manner maxim disregarded, especially in chat rooms where all the participants are 'talking at once' or Web pages where navigation is unclear. And lack of relevance has been a major issue when people use a search engine and find that the 'hits' are not what they wanted. In short, there's a great deal of uncooperativeness on the Internet, and in social media forums it's a common experience these days to find ourselves involved in an unpalatable conversation from which it's difficult to escape.

Pragmatic disorders

A rather different situation exists where the maxims can't be achieved because of a medical or psychological condition affecting language use. In clinical linguistics, the examples most often cited are from people who are unable to carry on a normal conversation, even though they have the technical linguistic skills—the pronunciation, grammar, and vocabulary—to do it. They're described as having *pragmatic* problems, with severe cases being referred to as *pragmatic disorders.*

The definition of pragmatics I gave in Chapter 1 was: the study of the choices—appropriate or inappropriate—we make when we use language in different situations, the reasons for those choices, and the effects that those choices convey. On this basis, people who have pragmatic problems in relation to language are either unable to make choices, or they make the wrong choices in a situation, or they are unable to respond appropriately to the choices others have made when communicating with them.

The condition is surprisingly common. Anyone who suffers from a language disability, no matter how minor, is going to be (at the very least) self-conscious about their ability, or lack of ability, to communicate; and when we reflect on the range of disabilities that exist, the likelihood of encountering someone with a pragmatic difficulty—in terms of this book, someone who is unable to carry on a normal conversation, or who makes it difficult for their listeners to respond in a normal way—is quite high. They include those who stammer, those who have suffered strokes or other brain damage that affects the brain's language centres, those who are unable to talk properly because of some paralysis or interference with articulation or voice production, and those who are suffering from some deterioration in mental ability, as in dementia. They also include those who have difficulty in forming normal personal relationships, as in the autistic spectrum, and children who have delayed or deviant language development. Dyslexia is included too: although this is defined as a problem of reading and writing, speaking and listening may also be affected. It's often possible to suspect that someone has a dyslexic history if they speak excessively and loudly, as if compensating for their literacy problem, but in the process making it difficult for their listeners to respond or maintain interest. There's a tendency to over-answer—to say more than is needed, and to go into details that strain the patience of the listener.

Then there's a group who seem to have nothing wrong with them at all. They may have above-average intelligence and good social skills, and yet in conversation we sense that all is not as it should be. Here are some of my own experiences. I was observing a speech therapy session in a school clinic room between a therapist and a child. There was a knock on the door. 'Come in,' said the therapist, and a girl of about 9 entered. It was the therapist's next patient, but she was early. 'Hello, Jane,' said the therapist, 'Sit there for a minute, will you?' Jane sat on the chair, and looked at her watch. She waited for exactly one minute, and then got up and left the room. The therapist had to get up and call her back in, and Jane sat there, a mite confused.

It's a common symptom in children who have a pragmatic problem: an idiom is taken literally. On another occasion a child came home asking her mother for sausages 'because her teacher was hungry'. Upon enquiry it transpired that the teacher had said, in response to someone asking her if she had any spare pencils, that she 'hadn't got a sausage'. Idioms being so common in everyday conversation, we have to be very careful to monitor responses when talking to children or adults who have pragmatic problems.

On yet another occasion I was due to visit a school for children with special linguistic needs. The headteacher had sent a boy (aged about 12) to meet me in the car park and show me the way in. We met, but he didn't reply to my greeting, or say anything until we were walking along a corridor. Then out of the blue he asked: 'Do you like being married?' Introducing a topic without a context, having no sense of which topics are (in)appropriate, or shifting topics without warning are other common pragmatic symptoms.

Conversations can be extremely difficult when topic shifts take place. It can be impossible to follow the train of thought, or to know how best to respond to it. Here's an example from a man who had suffered a traumatic brain injury, reported by Michael R. Perkins in an article on pragmatic impairment in the *Handbook of Clinical*

Linguistics (2008, p. 82). He can speak well enough in terms of pronunciation, grammar, and vocabulary—indeed, one might well call him fluent—but there is little sense in what he is saying due to the sudden changes in topic.

> I have got faults and . my biggest fault is . I do enjoy sport . it's
> something that I've always done . I've done it all my life . I've nothing
> but respect for my mother and father and . my sister . and basically
> sir . I've only come to this conclusion this last two months . and .
> as far as I'm concerned . my sister doesn't exist

The problem is difficult to diagnose. The erratic sequencing may be the result of reduced short-term memory—he forgets what he has just been talking about—or a difficulty with forward planning, or a perseveration with 'safe' familiar topics, or any combination of these. Whatever the reason, it is a hugely difficult situation for listeners, and especially for partners and therapists. Should they let him 'ramble on' with random and 'safe' autobiographical recollections or should they home in on one point and try to get him to focus, or introduce a fresh direction to the conversation that he and the listener might be able to control? To accept or to challenge, that is the question.

There is more coherence in this next example, from a 10-year-old (P) talking to his teacher (T), reported by Michael McTear (in *Children's Conversation*, 1985, Chapter 9), but the evasion and self-contradiction are confusing:

> T: which race would you like to be in?
> P: I like to be in X [*a town several miles from the school*] in the
>   sports day
> T: in X?
> P: yes
> T: what do you mean?
> P: I mean something
> T: is there a sports day in X?
> P: there is not, there is a sports day in Y [*at his school*]

T: then what's X got to do with it?
P: nothing
T: then why did you mention it?
P: indeed I did mention it
T: why did you mention it?
P: I don't know

And a third example, again from Michael Perkins' article—this time from a 5-year-old talking to his therapist:

T: could you eat that? [*indicating picture of oranges*]
P: no
T: why's that?
P: because the orange is hurting me
T: how does it hurt you?
P: he won't eat it
T: you don't eat oranges?
P: no
T: why not, John?
P: because silly
T: why are they silly?
P: an orange

Here coherence is complicated by a shifting of reference—from *me* to *he*, and the use of a present tense which should clearly be past. Pronouns often shift in this way, making it difficult for a listener to follow who is being referred to, especially when a story is being told. Nor does a listener immediately know how to respond. Normally, when someone introduces a new topic, there's an expectation that this will be explored in some way; but here, the therapist's taking up of the new topic ('silliness') gets her nowhere.

In all these instances, the frequency of T questions is notable, making dialogues in these situations very unlike normal everyday conversation. The Ps ask no questions—part of a generally observed reluctance to initiate a conversation or to keep one going. There may be a corresponding reluctance to respond, so that long silences enter into conversations. Often it's necessary for listeners to be extremely patient. With someone suffering from dementia, for example, a response to a question may be forthcoming, but only after some time. And when it does come it may be only distantly related to the question.

The variety of pragmatic symptoms is bewildering. Ps might ask a question and then answer it themselves. Or they might ask a question because they feel it is the right thing to do without really having any interest in the answer. Or they might echo the speaker's question, repeating it as if it were an answer. Echoing and repetition are among the commonest behaviours, especially when there is little or no comprehension. Ironically, one of the most important features of normal conversation—simultaneous feedback—may be used frequently, but inappropriately. P feels it is important to make affirming noises, without really following what is being said. Listeners can be fooled into thinking that all is well, conversationally, when it is far from being the case.

A recent study of adolescents with high functioning autistic spectrum disorder (HF-ASD), carried out by a team of speech and language therapists from the National University of Ireland (see p. 197), was headed: 'Just trying to talk to people... It's the hardest.' It shows how all the characteristics of conversation described in this book can be affected. The authors summarize earlier studies in this way:

> People with HF-ASD commonly exhibit difficulties with recognizing nuances of conversation, turn-taking, understanding humour and non-literal language, reciprocal conversation, following rules of politeness, knowing how to begin and end a conversation, and adjusting their language to meet the needs of the listener. ... They may have a restricted repertoire of interests and perseverate on topics that are of great interest to them. ... the frequency of abrupt topic shifts declines while interruptions increase in frequency.

There are many echoes here of the topics covered in my earlier chapters. An important point is that ASD adolescents are well aware of the pragmatic rules being broken—hence the title of the paper—as shown by quotations from some of the children studied. Jack, for example, aged 17, has a particular problem initiating a conversation:

> Well like unless someone starts first and it's something I'm interested in then it's not going to really work out.

Cian, also aged 17, finds topic choice especially problematic:

> it's just what to talk about is my main, you know, difficulty.

All expressed a wish for help to improve their social communication skills. One of the group interviewed wanted to develop a greater understanding about the way his conversation differed from that of other adolescents without ASD. Maria, aged 15, commented that 'it would be helpful if someone could like just write a guidebook' about communication. And the speech therapy team review various techniques that can help, such as building self-confidence through a peer mentor system, in which an ASD child has scheduled conversational sessions with a non-ASD schoolmate.

These examples only scratch the surface of the nature of pragmatic disability; but they are enough to show how the norms of everyday conversation can be seriously disturbed. In clinical and educational contexts pragmatic problems have in recent years been the focus of a great deal of research into the diagnosis, assessment, and treatment of the condition. And for students of conversation in general there has been an unexpected benefit, for the study of disability can draw our attention to features of normal everyday conversation that might otherwise be neglected, and in so doing shed fresh light on those norms.

The father of it all

Conversational maxims have been recognized for centuries. In the first century BC, Marcus Tullius Cicero wrote about conversation in Book 1 of his treatise *De Officiis* ('On Duty', translation here by Andrew Peabody, 1887). In point 37 he observed:

> The rhetoricians give rules for oratory; there are none for conversation. Yet I know not but that conversation might also have its rules.

And in the text that follows (divided below into paragraphs) he shows himself to be the father of present-day conversation analysis:

> Let then conversation, in which the followers of Socrates are preeminent, be easy, and by no means prolix; let politeness be always observed, nor must one debar others from their part, as if he had sole right to be heard; but, as in all things else, so in social intercourse, let him regard alternation as not unfair.
>
> Then, too, let him at the outset consider on what sort of subjects he is talking; if on serious things, let him show due gravity; on amusing, grace. Especially let him take heed lest his conversation betray some defect in his moral character, which is most frequently the case when the absent are expressly ridiculed or spoken of slanderously and malignly, with the purpose of injuring their reputation.
>
> For the most part, conversation relates to private affairs, or politics, or the theory and practice of the arts. Pains must then be taken that, if the conversation begins to wander off to other subjects, it be recalled to these. Yet reference must be had to

the persons present; for we are not all interested in the same things, at all times, and in a similar degree.

We should always observe, also, the length of time to which the pleasure of conversation extends, and as there was reason for beginning, so let there be a limit at which there shall be an ending.

Chapter Seventeen

DOES CONVERSATION CHANGE?

Most of the examples of real-world (as opposed to literary) conversation come from the recordings I made in the 1970s. That's fifty years ago. And it raises the obvious question: has conversational practice changed since then? Are people in the early decades of the twenty-first century discoursing in the same way? There are now several online collections of conversations that allow us to make a judgement. For example, the Santa Barbara Corpus of Spoken American English, released between 2000 and 2005, contains conversations such as this one, a 25-minute recording made at dinner-time at someone's home in California, and headed 'New Yorkers Anonymous' on their website. We see two of the four people present in this extract, which can be heard and read online (see p. 197). (I've simplified and adapted their detailed transcription to match the ones I've used earlier in this book, with an asterisk showing overlapping speech.)

FRAN: well I went to this church / and this is very interest*ing /
SEAN: *this is in Meridia /
FRAN: Merida /
SEAN: Merida / *that's right /
FRAN: *in the Yucatan / and it's lovely / – the people are sweet and nice / they're little / . they're dark / they all wear white / – and the city is quite nice / . it's a very manageable size . Merida / you can
(SEAN: unhunh) . you know /
SEAN: *walk everywhere /

FRAN: *walk around a lot / and you know / i i it's really lovely / – and
uh . anyway / I wen – and th . and the twine makers / the jute
industry was very big there at one time / . and the cemetery /
. there's a . there was . I don't know if it was called a labor
union / but some kind of association . uh . of twine makers /
were uh buried together / they had a section in the cemetery /
. and carved in marble / . and then painted / garish colors /
like aqua / and yellow / and everything / – but carved in stone
is these . ropes all around the – the various graves / and great
knots and things / – and but it all carved in stone / and then
painted / – your basic Mexican . house paint? / – you know /
(SEAN: yeah) all those colors? / yellow / (nice bright) and aqua
/ and pink / and you know /
(SEAN: nice bright colors /) green / . you know that green? / .
and it's a wonderful place / …

It's only a short extract (1.03 mins), but it displays all the conversational features described earlier, especially in Chapter 8. We have a
long turn from Fran, punctuated by short remarks from Sean (and
later from the other listeners). Sean provides simultaneous feedback
(*unhunh, yeah*), even at one point finishing off one of Fran's utterances (*walk everywhere*). Fran tells most of her story in short
intonational units: average words per unit (ignoring incomplete
utterances) is 4—which is a bit lower than the norm described on
p. 103, but explicable here because lists (as in *yellow / and aqua / and
pink / …*) tend to have shorter units. We hear comment clauses (*you
know*), fuzziness (*some kind of…, and things*), added interest through
adjectives and adverbs (*really lovely, great knots, wonderful place*),
self-repetitions (*it's lovely…it's really lovely; and then painted…and then
painted; aqua…and aqua*), and uptalk (shown by the two question marks
towards the end of the extract). In short, apart from the American
accents, this could just as easily be a story told by Tony or Gerry.

This shouldn't be a surprise. A quick glance back at the conversations I illustrated in Chapters 2 and 3 from Old, Middle, and Early
Modern English suggests that things haven't changed very much

over the centuries, let alone in the last fifty years. Individual words, idioms, spellings, and points of grammar may have dated, but the conversational dynamic we read in, say, Swift's *Polite Conversation* (p. 10) wouldn't be very different from what we would hear in a modern salon. However, the greater diversity of contexts and participants that can be found in modern corpora is something for which there is no precedent in literature, or even in the collections of spontaneous spoken English made by the first corpus projects. I recall transcribing a few confrontations from BBC debates, for the Survey of English Usage, but these were always polite and restrained. And there is nothing in *Advanced Conversational English* to illustrate the kind of furious row that is the stock-in-trade of TV soaps such as *Eastenders*, or the kind of rapid give-and-take that can be heard in a group of modern youngsters, with frequent interruptions and overlapping speech. Doubtless rows, interruptions, and overlaps were common enough in the days of Swift and Ælfric, but they would never have been written down.

The new corpora have begun to fill this gap. Listening to the wide range of recordings in the Santa Barbara corpus, we can hear family arguments...parent vs teenager rows...chat before, during, and after meals...people on the street, in a restaurant, in bed...serious conversations in offices, surgeries, and retail stores...playful talk at birthdays and Christmas...and much more. Here's a fragment from a recording headed 'Stay out of it'—a bad-tempered exchange between a mother and daughter which, I suspect, will be immediately recognized by anyone who has gone through this phase of family relationships (or is an *Eastenders* addict).

SANDRA: how am I supposed to know when you're telling the truth /
MARY: that was a joke / that was a joke /
SANDRA: yeah / and I'm supposed to read your mind and know what you're joking about /
MARY: no / but it was a joke /
SANDRA: you know / Mary / I don't know how many times I gotta tell you...

Looking at an entire transcript, we don't see any of the leisurely story-telling described in earlier chapters. We see short utterances, awkward silences, speakers not being allowed to finish, a point being repeatedly made, accusations of 'you're not listening', sporadic name-calling or obscenities, and a general shapelessness as the row meanders backwards and forwards until the participants decide to call it a day or one of them leaves the room. In this respect, the tightly scripted quarrels on television are untypical. Writers need to move the story on, whereas in non-TV domestic settings the arguments can go round and round indefinitely, or begin again without change after a break. 'Round 2', a dispassionate observer might remark.

Does the stylistic diversity presented by a modern corpus bring to light any linguistic novelties? On the whole, the conversations look reassuringly familiar. But when we encounter extracts such as the following, also based on the Santa Barbara corpus, we realize that—for some speakers in some settings—times have changed. Here are two illustrations.

Novelty 1: like

This is from 'Just Wanna Hang', a face-to-face conversation between four female university students, aged 20 or 21, sharing an apartment in Vermont. One is describing what happened when she and her family left a restaurant the night before (for those unfamiliar with American high-school or university terminology, a sophomore is a second-year student):

> ARIANNA: we're leaving / and the guy's like . we left a little bit .
> ahead of my parents? / – and the guy's like, hi you guys /
> – how was your dinner / and we were like great / thinking
> you know he was just asking us how our dinner was / –
> he's like . yeah you know going on about / w– what are you /
> sophomores, / we're like no / . but everyone at . thinks
> we're like young? /

DANA: ah
ARIANNA: so we were like no / seniors / . then he goes / well – / we're
           looking for part time help / – like he was just like recruit-
           ing us / right *off of the dinner table /
NANCY: *mm /
DANA: that's so great *though /
ARIANNA: *isn't that awesome /

American commentators say that this kind of monologue, with its frequent use of *like*, was coming into fashion, especially in California, in the 1970s, but there was no sign of it then among young people in the UK. It was another couple of decades before its presence in American films and TV shows produced a corresponding increase in British usage. Any present-day recording of a conversation between people of a similar age outside the USA would bring to light many such examples—and the reaction among older people to its overuse has been predictably fierce, especially when youngsters are encountered who are unable to moderate its use when speaking in more formal situations.

What is always missed, when criticisms are made, is the way *like* is being used with a range of different functions. Its chief use, illustrated by almost all of Arianna's instances, is to introduce a quotation—what linguists call a *quotative*. If I were to write out the conversation as a dialogue in a novel, it would go something like this:

'Hi, you guys. How was your dinner?', asked the owner.
'Great,' Arianna replied.
'What are you? Sophomores?'
'No.' Arianna knew that everyone thought they looked young.
'No, seniors,' she added.
'Well, we're looking for part-time help.'

Like in effect replaces the quotation marks:

LIKE Hi, you guys. How was your dinner?
LIKE Great.

LIKE What are you? Sophomores?
LIKE No.
LIKE No, seniors.

But this isn't the whole story of *like*. It doesn't explain these three instances:

but everyone at . thinks we're like young?
like he was just like recruiting us

Here we see *like* being used to introduce a word or utterance that the speaker thinks needs special focus, usually because it's a vivid or dramatic expression. *Recruiting* is just such a word—unexpected in this context, and thus likely to be appreciated as a clever metaphor. The utterance as a whole—*recruiting us right off of the dinner table*—is similarly creative, for *recruit* doesn't normally collocate (p. 108) with *dinner table*. So we get a double use of *like*, drawing the listener's attention to the expression that is about to follow. The first instance introduces the sentence as a whole; the second introduces the metaphor. *Like*, in effect, is saying: 'Pay attention to what I think is a nice piece of creative language, and I hope you think so too.'

Like thus adds an element of exclamatory force to what is about to be said, and this also explains its use before *young*. Arianna wants to give a reason for the owner's reaction to her friends, and *like* identifies the crucial word. Here, there's no element of surprise because evidently her friends all know they look young. Why evidently? Because *young* is spoken with a rising tone (shown by the question mark). It is uptalk (p. 88), used here as a request for confirmation—and it is acknowledged by Dana's *ah*. (There's a second instance of uptalk in the extract: *We left a little bit ahead of my parents?* That's a nice example of a comprehension check: Arianna simply wants to make it clear that the young people were on their own when the event happened. It doesn't require a response.)

This by no means exhausts the various functions *like* has in narrative. As well as focusing on a word or phrase, it can be used to challenge it. If I say *The table was like—rectangular*, I'm saying that the word *rectangular* isn't an exact fit, but it's the best I can do for the moment. Linguists call this *hedging*—not giving full commitment to what is about to be said. It's similar in its role to *sort of, kind of, more or less*, and other such expressions of fuzziness. And it is this sense of approximation that we find in older, related uses, such as in Jerome K. Jerome's *Three Men in a Boat* (1889, Chapter 15):

> We had had a sail—a good all-round exciting, interesting sail—and now we thought we would have a row, just for a change like.

This utterance-final use of *like* is widespread in regional dialects, where it's by no means restricted to young people. I heard it all the time from adults when I was a teenager in Liverpool, and it's conversationally common where I live now, in Wales, and in Irish and Scottish English too.

Novelty 2: so

Pedantic complaints are usually pointers to language change, and the greater the ferocity of the complaint, the more likely that we are encountering a genuine shift in usage. When we find a British media pundit like John Humphrys attacking the word *so*, when used at the beginning of a sentence, as a 'noxious weed', 'irritating', and 'absurd', and saying that people who use it are 'linguistic vandals', we know that a real change must be going on. He said all this in a piece he wrote for *Waitrose Weekend* magazine in 2015, and his view was supported by a huge number of responses to the BBC *Feedback* programme of the time. Is this a new conversational feature, as is claimed?

Humphrys was thinking mainly of people interviewed on such programmes as BBC's *Today*, who would answer a question like this:

INTERVIEWER: Were you at the meeting, minister?
MINISTER: So, there were a number of meetings...

The critical consensus was that such a usage makes speakers sound evasive, or pseudo-intellectual, and reduces their credibility. It has been described as a 'lazy' alternative to *er, um, well,* and other fillers that provide a moment of extra thinking time before they reply. But the criticism extends to writing as well as speech, where *so* is condemned if it adds nothing to the meaning of the sentence it introduces—where it is omissible (and where it *should* be omitted according to the pedants). Examples like the following illustrate where each instance of *so* could be omitted without the rest of the sentence being affected. The writer is criticizing the overuse of the word *respect*:

> So does this all mean that we now have more not only of the word but also of what it represents?

and two paragraphs later:

> So it may be that much of this talk of 'respect' is no more than waving the word about.

and then after some quotations:

> So what exactly is going on here?

I'm being naughty, as these are all taken from three pages in Chapter 8 of *Beyond Words* (2008), written by, er, John Humphrys.

It's easy enough to hoist pedants by their own petard; but this doesn't address the question of why a usage like *so* has attracted such criticism. For in fact there's nothing new about it, other than its increased presence in the public ear on radio and television. The use of omissible *so* as an introductory particle, beginning a conversational turn without any clear meaning, and usually followed by a comma in writing or a potential pause in speech, can be traced back at least to Shakespeare. Here's Queen Isabel beginning a speech in *Richard II* (2.2.62):

> So, Green, thou art the midwife to my woe

Its use in everyday conversation must have been frequent in the years that followed, otherwise why should Swift satirize it as one of the features of upper-class speech in his *Polite Conversation*? This is Sir John Linger talking to Colonel Atwit:

> I'Faith, one of your finical *London* Blades dined with me last year in *Derbyshire*: So, after Dinner, I took a Pipe: So, my Gentleman turn'd away his Head: So, said I, what Sir, do you never smoak? So, he answered as you do, Colonel, no; but I sometimes take a Pipe: So, he took a Pipe in his Hand, and fiddled with it, 'till he broke it: So, said I, pray, Sir, can you make a Pipe? So, he said, no: So, said I, why then, Sir, if you can't make a Pipe, you should not break a Pipe. So, we all laught.

Leaving aside the exaggerated use, these are all ways of managing the conversation—linking pieces of narrative, and showing how the story continues. It's basically telling us: listen to what's about to be said, as it's going to be of particular relevance to my story.

What is of relevance may well be an extra bit of explanation—a backstory, as writers on narrative technique put it. American linguist Geoff Nunberg sums it up nicely in a podcast on NPR (3 September 2015):

> I go to the Apple Store and ask the guy at the Genius Bar why my laptop is running slow. He starts by saying, 'So, Macs have two kinds of disk permissions...' If that 'so' were a chapter title in a Victorian novel, it would read, 'In which it is explained what the reader must know before his question can be given a proper answer.'

Exactly. This use of *so* tells the listener that the issues are more complex than the questioner might expect. It's therefore likely to be more common in conversations of a specialized, technical, or academic kind. I can imagine some interviewees on the *Today* programme, having been asked a question that they know is facile or intended to trip them up, taking a deep breath as they say *So*... Of course, Humphrys is right some of the time: a *so*-user can use it to change the subject and thus evade the question, while giving the impression that the answer is relevant. And if someone were to use it after a really simple and uncontentious question, it could indeed warrant the sneer of 'pseudo-intellectual'. But that won't explain all of its functions.

It won't explain, for example, its use in the Arianna conversation, where at one point, after a pause, one of the participants says, as they work out what to do with the rest of their evening:

so / what's the plan /

Imagine if she had just said, after a pause:

what's the plan /

It sounds more abrupt, more out of the blue. The *so* softens the stylistic force, and suggests that there has already been some discussion about what to do next. 'What were we talking about?' It's a 'resume' function, which can also be seen in this piece of dialogue from *Advanced Conversational English* (Recording 6). Mary has been describing where her house is in London, and Evelyn interrupts:

MARY: our house / . er leads straight down to the – / well / right into the heart of Little Venice / which is beautiful / – I mean / in I hadn't realized / how absolutely lovely it is /
EVELYN: is Little Venice where the canal ends /
MARY: yes /
EVELYN [*laughs*]: it sounds as though it did /
MARY: so the canal runs / at the end of our road /...

Mary clearly wants the topic to return to where her house is, and the *so* tells Evelyn that what she is about to say runs on from what she was saying before. It's a friendly way of telling the listener: you shouldn't have interrupted me, as I was in the middle of a story. This use of *so* is often reinforced by another 'resuming' word. Recording 8 begins:

so anyway / all went well / . . .

It can be an especially useful word when a conversation has lapsed into silence. I recall one instance in a foursome where, after a conversation stopper (p. 51), one of the speakers looks around at the others and says *so*, in a jocular way. He says nothing else, waiting for someone else to say something, and one of the others then does. It fills the gap, and helps to reduce any awkwardness.

Then there are several dramatic or literary uses of *so*.

o Joke-telling often begins with it:
   So this penguin walks into a bar...

o A blog or post can begin with it—indeed, I discover online that a blogger named John D. Ratelif begins every one of his blog posts with *So*...

o A TV programme title can begin with it:
   So Haunt Me (BBC1, 1992–4)
   So What Now? (BBC1, 2001)
   So You Think You Can Dance (Fox TV, 2005–)

o An everyday story often begins with it:
   So I was walking down this street...

o And one of the most famous literary stories of all is made to begin with it—in Seamus Heaney's translation of the opening lines of *Beowulf*:
   So. The Spear-Danes in days gone by
   And the kings who ruled them had courage and greatness.

He comments that this use 'obliterates all previous discourse and narrative, and at the same time functions as an exclamation calling for immediate attention'. And it's perhaps no surprise that he opted for this solution, given his Irish background, for an initial *so* is well established in everyday Hiberno-English, turn-initially, -medially, and -finally:

So how's it going?
[There's Mike.] Ah yes, there's Mike, so it is.
[Are you going to the shop?] I am, so.

Clearly, there's far more to the use of *so* than it being simply, as some pundits have claimed, a filler word that gives the speaker some extra thinking time, like a *well* or a voiced hesitation (*er*, *erm*).

So, yes, English conversation is changing, in that a few features are being used by some speakers apparently with much greater frequency than they used to be, and are altering its character. I say 'apparently' because we don't know how they were being used in the days before the rise of mass media made these usages more audible and before recordings of everyday informal English became available. Observations such as Swift's suggest that some of them might have been more common than the literary record suggests. Future linguistic historians will have a much easier time, as they will be able to mine online databases for data on current trends.

New openings, reactions, and closings

While the internal structure of a conversation seems to have changed little over the centuries, the way we open and close a conversation has developed in noticeable ways. Among the turn-closings these days we hear such expressions as *That's the thing* or *right?* (as in *I know, right?*), as well as conversation closings such as *Take care, Laters, Catch you later,* and *See you later*—the latter still disturbing older listeners who are used to the word *later* meaning 'on the same day'. Aficionados of *The Prisoner* (p. 41) tend to say *Be seeing you*.

Fashionable topic reactions include *wow, yay, no way, oh my god, absolutely* replacing *yes,* and (when acknowledging an enjoyable experience) *you guys!,* and *innit.* This last one has attracted most media comment, as it has, in a short space of time, evolved a wide range of functions. Although etymologically a colloquial pronunciation of third person *isn't it,* it became an invariant tag question (like *n'est-ce pas* in French), so that we hear first and second person *I'm going, innit* and *You're going, innit.* The function, as with traditional tag questions, is to get the listener to agree, verify, or corroborate something that's just been said. But when we hear it in a narrative like this one, something else is going on:

> . . . so he gave me his keys / innit / and I went down to the garage
> by your place / innit / and . . .

The tag is now acting as a conversational filler like *you know* or *you see.* It's helping the narrative to flow, and building rapport, as *innit* is basically saying 'you know what I'm talking about'. It can even be used on its own:

TOM: that was a great game /
HARRY: innit /

Here it's simply an expression of agreement.

Conversational openings change too. They always have. Early twentieth-century novels and music-hall repartee show us openings that are no longer with us, such as *I say* (though perhaps still used in upper-class circles?), and *I say, I say, I say*... Future linguistic historians of the present day will note the arrival of *hi* replacing *hello*, and the increased use of *hey*, especially when used as a wake word when talking to a machine:

Hey Siri...
Hey Google...

That brings us into a whole new conversational world.

Chapter Eighteen

#ALMOST DONE

It won't be long before we get analyses of conversations with Siri, Alexa, and their colleagues. Most people feel they change the way they speak when talking to a virtual assistant, especially when they have to repeat a question because the application has failed. And the rhythm of the conversation changes. There's always a gap between the end of a question and the assistant's response because of the processing time involved. The gap can be quite long if extra time is needed to understand a regional accent, or the enquirer is speaking too fast, or the question is too long and involved or uses a little-known proper name. Huge progress has been made with speech recognition software, so that conversations with machines are now a lot more natural-sounding than they were even a decade ago; but we are still a long way behind the kind of dialogue we hear when Dave Bowman talks to HAL in *2001*.

> HAL: By the way, do you mind if I ask you a personal question?
> DAVE: No, not at all.
> HAL: Well, forgive me for being so inquisitive; but during the past few weeks, I've wondered whether you might be having some second thoughts about the mission.
> DAVE: How do you mean?
> HAL: Well, it's rather difficult to define.

At the same time, we are a long way ahead of the typing interaction that was the norm in the early days of human–computer interaction, and found in fiction such as David Lodge's *Small World* (p. 119).

There used to be only two sides to this interaction: us communicating with the machine, and the machine communicating with us. Today there's a third side: us talking with each other online, using the services of a machine. The term *conversation* has further extended to include an enormous range of interactions, such as by email, in chat rooms, and on social media sites such as Twitter, Facebook, Snapchat, and Instagram. The history of online conversation is littered with the corpses of old networks—Friendster, Friends Reunited, Piczo, Heello...—and relics of old linguistic conventions. When I first began to study online chat and games, in the 1990s, it was full of locutions such as:

Doc looks horrified
Prof grins
Doc eyes Prof warily

Emoticons and emojis have largely taken over those functions today, though we do still see alerts in the third person, such as 'Matthew is typing'.

Digitally mediated conversation has evolved as an online counterpart to face-to-face speech, with just a few differences. In Chapter 14 I was chiefly concerned to discuss the things that are missing in online chat, such as simultaneous feedback. But that is only half the story. The informal writing we see in social media forums has added an array of new conventions to conversational practice. A prime illustration is the use of the symbol #, which has gone under a variety of names, such as *hash, mesh, sharp, crunch, hex, flash, gate, octothorpe, pound*, but is now most often encountered as *hashtag*.

Hashtags

Hashtags began on Twitter in 2007 as a way (a *tag*) of classifying content so that people could find all the tweets relating to a particular topic. So we might find, at the end of a message about the result of a tennis match, or about a tennis star, *#tennis*. Similarly, if anyone wanted to find all the tweets that had been sent relating to a favourite TV show, they would appear together by searching for *#doctorwho*, *#gameofthrones*, or whatever. Surveys suggest around three-quarters of those who use social media regularly put hashtags into their posts, though patterns of usage vary. A survey by Trackmaven in 2016 found Twitter and Facebook posts mainly using just one or two hashtags per post, whereas on Instagram the popular frequency was ten or more. The range of topics hashtagged is enormous, as the device is used to identify any item or person of interest, and thus includes advertising campaigns, business conferences, holiday destinations, or any name or word that a writer thinks is of general interest.

The convention was seen not only as a convenient search facility. It was also a means of starting or continuing a conversation about a topic of shared interest. It was the universal conversation opener. Advertisers picked up on it in the form of a 'Twitter party', usually sponsored by a brand or a website: a hashtag identifier invites people to go online at a certain time to talk about something—as one website put it, 'like a meet-and-greet you'd have in a physical store'. Social media jargon introduced the notion of *engagement*: the more hashtags, the more engagement, as measured, for example, by the number of times a message gets sent on to others (*retweeted*).

That, at least, was how the convention began. But within a few years its function widened: it began to identify a more general comment or attitude, displaying only an indirect relationship to the content of the post. For example, a post I received recently announced the engagement of a couple, and the sender ended it with *#delighted*. It's an interesting development. If I write *#delighted*, I am subtly (and succinctly) altering my viewpoint. Instead of meaning simply 'I am delighted', I mean something like 'Look at me being delighted, and I'm offering you the chance to agree'. Tweets from other people may then affirm your view, by attaching *#delighted* to their posts. Social media pundits have described this use in various ways. It adds a third person perspective to what would otherwise be a first person text.

It introduces a degree of distance between the writer and the content. With some instances, there is clearly a tone of irony or self-deprecation—as might be conveyed by a wry emoticon or emoji. Its brevity is part of its appeal.

Then, as so often happens with new linguistic conventions, people began to play with hashtags. Longer phrases were hashtagged, such as *#ihopeyoulikeit* on Instagram, where the context is an unimaginably diverse group of pictures. In each case, viewers can give a conversational response in the form of a 'like/unlike' vote. Another message announces the impending publication of a song, and adds

#scared #excited #mostly scared #ihopeyoulikeit

Hashtag inflation was the result of this trend, with some posts containing as many hashtags as would fit into the space provided with minimal explanation. And then, the surprising thing happened: social forum users offline began to introduce the online convention into their face-to-face conversation[s?]. Here's an example:

we're gonna miss the bus—hashtag it's time to go

The speaker finds it witty, knowing that his listeners do it too. It's a bonding feature: it affirms that they all hang out together on social media. But in these examples, something more is going on:

I know I should have bought one—hashtag sorry
yeah I saw it—hashtag brilliant

Here the speakers are being ironic. The first speaker is not really sorry. The second doesn't really think the programme was brilliant. It's the distancing effect again: the hashtag is saying to the listener, 'I don't really mean this'. It's often said in a lower tone of voice.

Then there's a cluster of uses where the function is more like *so*, *like*, or *innit*, discussed in the previous chapter. I'm not sure how else to explain someone who arrives in a room and says *hashtag hi*. And in this next example, the usage is clearly marking a topic shift, similar to the 'resuming' function of *so*. There's been a pause in the conversation, when someone says:

hashtag let's go see a movie.

The effect is different from saying simply: *let's go see a movie.* That version expresses the speaker's personal wish. The hashtag version is more nuanced: it says, in effect, 'what do you think about the idea of going to see a movie?' If it were online, it would receive a set of likes or dislikes from the poster's contacts.

It's been noticed that some people who say *hashtag* also accompany it with a crossed fingers gesture, mimicking the graphic shape of the symbol. This kind of non-verbal communication is a familiar strategy, often seen in face-to-face conversation when someone mimics inverted commas while saying a word by raising a hand on either side of their head, palm outward, and wiggling their first two fingers. And it's this combination of words and gestures that has appealed to the comedians who, very soon after the usage began to spread, pilloried it in pastiches of everyday conversation in which virtually every sentence begins with a gesture-accompanied 'hashtag'. Here's the opening of a skit in 2012 by the Irish comedy group Foil Arms and Hog:

ARMS: How's it going? Hashtag greeting.
HOG: Not too bad. How's your weekend? Hashtag just making conversation.
ARMS: Ah, just went out with Niamh you know—hashtag my new hot girlfriend.
HOG: Oh the old ball and chain, eh—hashtag it should have been me—hashtag keep it together now...

And so it continues. A year later, the same kind of parody turns up in a fast-moving conversation on *The Tonight Show Starring Jimmy Fallon* between Jimmy Fallon and Justin Timberlake. Both are viewable on YouTube (p. 198).

Generation gaps

Some commentators were surprised when they saw *hashtag* being used in this way, but they shouldn't have been. Some were appalled, thinking that online conversational features should stay online, and not be demeaned by being used in offline situations. But from the very beginning of electronic media, people have been taking online usage and adapting it for general conversational use. I made a collection of such instances in 2004, in my now hugely outdated *A Glossary of Netspeak and Textspeak*. Here are a few of them:

> Hey, backspace a minute! I want to go over that again.
> I wish I could help, but no bandwidth, sorry.
> Good point! I'll bookmark that for the next time I see her.
> My bike's down: it needs a new set of brake pads.
> Time for me to log off, guys. I'm getting tired.
> Sorry, working Saturdays isn't on my menu.
> I'll ping you later.
> Anyone seen the readme for the lawn-mower?

Similarly, we've seen in recent years how some of the abbreviations found in chats and texts have left their digital home and entered everyday speech, such as *LOL/lol* and *OMG*. This is parodied too in the *Tonight Show* clip, where one of the participants says *lolololololol*...instead of laughing.

Even online there have been changes in usage, and *lol* is a good example. It originally settled down with the meaning 'laughing out loud', after some uncertainty ('lots of love'). But it didn't take long for users to see that its literal meaning was a fiction. The word had become simply a marker of amusement, sometimes of irony or sarcasm. So when it became necessary to say that a message had indeed made the receiver laugh out loud, a new convention had to emerge. Some repeated the letters: *LOLOL* or *lolol*. Some glossed it: *actual lol*. And over the years, its use became more nuanced. American linguist Michelle McSweeney, after examining thousands of messages (see the online reference on p. 198), concluded that the use of *lol* was in fact restricted in its distribution. It's usually used just once in an utterance, typically at the end, and it tends to be used only when a topic needs to be ameliorated in some way, or made more empathetic—much as a friendly smiley is used at the end of an utterance. If the message is already full of empathy, it won't be there. So, for example, we will find the first of the following instances, not the second:

I really think you should get new specs lol
I really love you lol

The first *lol* suggests that the writer is making a jokey allusion to something. If the second were ever used, it would really be quite hurtful. And it's perhaps because of these subtle nuances that some messagers now avoid *lol* altogether, replacing it with *haha*, *hahaha*, and the like.

It really is quite remarkable how a linguistic change on the Internet can arrive, evolve new uses, and change its status in a matter of a few years, or even months. The point has been repeatedly noticed with reference to memes—notions that spread rapidly across a culture, often taking linguistic form, as with catchphrases. Some, such as *KEEP CALM AND . . .*, have lasted for years; others go out of fashion very quickly. But while they are alive, the Internet spreads them faster than any other possible method. How long the new convention will last is a matter of speculation, but when motivated by technological change, the effects are unlikely to be short-lived. In instant messaging conversations, for instance, there's the absence of a period after statements—a norm that now allows for an extra layer of meaning if someone chooses to put one in. For many young people (and increasingly among older), if a sentence reads:

Johnny will be there

it is a simple statement of fact. But if it reads

Johnny will be there.

it means something like 'Oh dear. I'm not looking forward to that'. Social media commentators have used the phrase *passive aggression* to describe cases like that.

Similarly, ellipsis dots (...) are traditionally used to show omission, separation, or incompleteness, without further nuance. If I write, informally:

> so three of us will go...John...probably Mark...and Jane... maybe others...

the dots express my hesitancy and separate my thoughts. I am much more in control if I write:

> so three of us will go: John, probably Mark, and Jane, maybe others.

In an instant message, the thought separation can be expressed by the simple process of adding a linebreak (shown by ^):

> so three of us will go^
> John^
> probably Mark^
> and Jane^
> maybe others^

This then allows a nuanced use of the dots. To write

> and Jane...

could suggest that something is being left unsaid about Jane. There's some sort of problem here, which the sender assumes the recipient will be aware of. To someone brought up on the older use of ellipsis dots, such a nuance would pass unnoticed, or perhaps it would be assumed that the writer has been inconsistent. But to many of the new generation(s) of Internet users, the dots speak volumes.

Gretchen McCulloch sums it up well in her *Because Internet* (2019, Chapter 4), using the example

> how's it going...

She comments:

> if you're solidly in the linebreak camp, you see those extra dots
> or even just a single period where a linebreak or a message break
> would have sufficed, and assume that anything that takes more
> effort than necessary is a potential message. The dots must be
> indicating something left unsaid: 'how's it going [there's some-
> thing I'm not telling you].' From a peer, something left unsaid
> might indicate flirtation. But from an older relative, that would
> be weird.

If I were the older relative, my dots would mean no more than wanting to show a continuative tone of voice. To me, it's more informal
than ending the question with a question mark. But it seems I might be
leaving my young relative puzzling over what I'm getting at. There
are differences between adults too. My wife, having read this para-
graph, commented that to her the dots mean 'I know there's been a
problem, maybe with you, and I'm being circumspect'.

I wonder just how much inter-generational confusion there is as
a result of the speed of language change on the Internet. Later in the
chapter, McCulloch adds a droll comment:

> there's a catch-22 when it comes to analyzing youth language:
> your intuitions about it are inversely proportional to your ability
> to write about it. I can assert things with confidence about the
> slang of the 1990s and 2000s, but as the 2010s continue, I'm
> already feeling myself slipping out of touch...

And here's me, trying to do the same thing at twice her age. It's time
for an Epilogue.

Epilogue

There's a feeling around that the practice of conversation is dying out. I see it in the title of Stephen Miller's *Conversation: a History of a Declining Art* (2006). And it's there in Theodore Zeldin's *Conversation: How Talk Can Change Our Lives* (1998, p. 3): 'the twenty-first century needs a new ambition, to develop not talk but conversation'. He's thinking of the kind of 'meeting of minds with different memories and habits' (p. 14) that we've seen repeatedly affirmed in writers such as Emerson and Johnson. But it's important not to over-intellectualize this view. There are different memories and habits evident in Gerry and Tony's conversation about football grounds, which is one of the most demotic of subjects. And I've often overheard groups of young-sters animatedly debating the qualities of the latest video game they'd been playing in the isolation of their bedrooms the day before, and comparing their experiences of other games they've played.

This is a repeat of the view that was often propounded in the 1970s: children are watching too much television, so their conversa-tional skills will be harmed. The prophets of doom failed to take into account the lively conversations taking place in the school play-ground the next day, discussing what had happened in the pro-gramme the night before. If there was any handicap at all, it was among the children who had *not* seen the programme and who thus found themselves less able to contribute. These children of the tele-vision generation are ageing adults now, and complaining with great fluency about the texting habits of the young.

The exchange of text messages, or their equivalent on WhatsApp and the various other forums, is a new kind of conversation, indeed, but it is nonetheless a conversation. The exchanges I've analysed over the years typically display fluency, intelligibility, and appropriateness—the latter reflecting identity as members of a particular social group (so not always in standard English). And they are conversing much more often than I did when I was their age. What is important is for messagers to be aware of the limitations as well as the strengths of the new medium, as I illustrated in Chapter 14. That is a task still facing schools, where there may be little or no instruction about the properties of electronic communication in all its forms.

I said in my Prologue that conversation has been described as an art, a mind-reading exercise, a game, a battle. None of these metaphors totally captures the multi-faceted character of everyday conversation. It can share some of the properties of art, in the sense of an aesthetic that provides insight and illumination to watching or listening observers, but it does more than art, for the observers are themselves participants in the creative process. Zeldin again:

> When minds meet, they don't just exchange facts: they transform them, reshape them, draw different implications from them, engage in new trains of thought. Conversation doesn't just reshuffle the cards: it creates new cards.

Nor is conversation really like a battle or game for there are no winners and losers. Admittedly, a conversation is sometimes a conflict between minds or wits, but more often it is a cooperative enterprise, with people seeking the same goal. The aim of a conversation, as writers have affirmed repeatedly (p. 77), is to make everyone feel happy or satisfied at the end of it—'a pleasing impression', as Dr Johnson put it. A book about conversation should do the same.

The football grounds conversation

/ shows the boundary of an intonation/rhythm unit
. shows a short pause
– shows a longer pause
* shows overlapping speech
( ) enclose simultaneous feedback

ANDY: well / what's the . what's the failure with the football /
I mean this . this I don't really see / I mean it . cos the money / .
how much does it cost *to get in / down the road / now /

GERRY: *I think it probably – it probably is the money / for what
you get / you know / – erm I was reading in the paper this morning / a a chap / he's a director / of a big company / in Birmingham /
– who was th the world's number one football fan / he used to
spend / about a thousand a year / watching football / you know /
(TONY: coo /) – he's he's watched football in every n . on every
league . ground in England / all ninety two / (ANDY *laughs*) – and
he's been to America / to watch West Bromwich playing in
America / he's . he's been to the la . to oh / . the last / f f two or
three world cup / . world cup / . mat things / you know / . tourna-
ments / – and he goes to all the matches away / you know /
European cup matches and everything / that English teams are
playing in / he's all over the world watching it you see / this year /
he's watched twenty two games / – so far / this year /which is about
. fifty per cent / of his normal / (TONY: good Lord /) . and even
he's getting browned off / and he was saying / that erm – you can
go to a nightclub / in Birmingham / – and watch Tony Bennett / .
for about thirty bob / – something like this / a night with Tony

Bennett / – have a nice meal / . in . very . plushy surroundings /
very warm / nice / pleasant / – says it costs him / about the same
amount of money / to go and sit in a breezy windy stand / – (ANDY
AND TONY *laugh*) on a . on a wooden bench / – to watch / a rather
boring game of football / with no personality / and all defensive /
and everything / he says it's just killing itself / you know / (ANDY:
yeah / TONY: m /) – they're not giving the entertainment they
used to give / the erm – conditions have / if anything / are not
are f deteriorated / and er (TONY: in what way /) they're charging
f three times what they used to / – or four times what they used
to /

TONY: in what way have conditions deteriorated Gerry /

GERRY: well the grounds / are scruffier than they used to be /
I mean they never do these grounds up / do they / I mean they're
progressively *getting worse /

TONY: *you know / I thought they always had these wooden
benches and stands *and that /

GERRY: *yeah / but they've been getting worse / I mean you don't –
er every now and again the team builds a new stand / (TONY: m /) .
I mean the stand that you sit in on most grounds now / is the very
same stand / – you sat in – thirty years ago / forty years ago /
(TONY: oh . / now / Gerry / i *coughs*) excepting it's probably
* deteriorated /

TONY: *but there was an interesti / you're quite right / there was
that one that collapsed (GERRY: yeah /) . but there was an interesting programme on these grounds / (GERRY *clears throat*) the way it
showed talked about the continental ones / that one it was it in
Madrid / . they're superb / (GERRY: oh / they're tremendous /) .
and the way they could clear them / in x number of seconds / – a
crowd of s s erm seventy thousand I think it was / out of one
ground / – they had . they had it s organized / in such a way / that
there was so many entrances all round / – m you know / . arcs /

like this / upstairs downstairs / – they're all . funnelled in such / – I
mean they'd all . pla . the passages / and exits / all planned / in such
a way / that everybody could get out / you know / – and erm . it
was after that disaster you know . (GERRY: Rangers /) I think he
said there was only one modern ground in England / really / that
could claim to be modern / was it Man City / – (GERRY: Coventry
maybe /) or was theirs taken as one of the oldest / – but you know /
it said – all ours / are really ancient / except . erm about one or two /
– compared with these continentals / – cos they're all built pu
they're purpose built / – for modern conditions / . and ours aren't / .
and every time a disaster like this happens / or somebody gets
killed in a . or trampled in a crush / – er a stand breaks / . this . erm
– this highlights it / and they sort of . patch it up / and it's botched /
you know / thi . because . I suppose it's alright / . easy to talk / but
if you've got . so many thousand quid's worth of – stand there /
you're not going to sort of knock it all down / and build it from
scratch / . you just patch it up / don't you / (GERRY: yeah /) . of
course / the continentals / I suppose / they came in late / and they .
build them – (GERRY: properly /) you know / this Milan ground / .
there's a famous one there isn't there / . (GERRY: erm) you know /
they were saying how superb they were / . but the one in Spain /
was the best / – (GERRY: of course) I thought it was in Madrid / –
was it Real Madrid / they were fan (GERRY: they're all erm) oh they
were fantastic / it showed the photographs of them / . people sitting there in the hot sun / you know / smoking cigars / and . out i
and it showed the crowds . emptying / – (GERRY: m /) they had a
practice – erm exit / (GERRY: yeah /) – you know / er – alarm / . oh /
it was fantastic / the speed that they got out /

GERRY: oh one minute there was . seventy thousand in the ground /
(TONY: yeah / yeah /) and about . thirty seconds later / or a minute
later *they were clear /

TONY: *you know about . I don't know / about twenty entrances /
(ANDY: yeah /) strategically placed / for top and bottom / you

know / all round the ground / . (GERRY: yeah /) – you know / like spokes from a wheel / they were out in no *time /

GERRY: *and they all went go / straight out of out of the gr . completely away from the place / (TONY: yeah / ANDY: m /) – oh / here in England / I mean you all come haring out / and then you all get into a f . a funnel / – about er (ANDY: oh yeah / a jam /) about as wide as . two . two normal drives I suppose / –

TONY: I went to Stamford Bridge last year *once /

GERRY: *all fifty thousand have got to get out through there /

TONY: I'd never been before / . cor / – cor / the crowds / . ooh / and you wondered / if you were going to be trampled to death / they started to shove / . do you know / it's quite frightening / (ANDY: where was this Tony / GERRY: yeah /) carrying Justin / – Stamford Bridge / where I went to see Chelsea / play Leeds / (ANDY: oh yes / m /) – and Leeds played shockingly / – worst game they ever played /

GERRY: well some of the gates might be about as wide as that room / as the room / mightn't they / *really /

TONY: *ooh / there were kids / sitting *on that great hoarding /

GERRY: *about as wide as that / – and about thirty thousand have to go out through there / (TONY: cor /) you know / I mean er (ANDY: m) – oh it's terrible /

TONY: ooh / the sea of – bodies in front of you moving / and people started to push / behind you / it got quite frightening / cos you couldn't have done anything you'd have been absolutely helpless /

References

Linguistic references

Perkins, M. R. 2008. Pragmatic impairment as an emergent phenomenon. In M. Ball, R. Perkins, N. Müller, & S. Howard (eds), *Handbook of Clinical Linguistics*. Oxford: Blackwell, 79–91.

Cameron, D. 2007. *The Myth of Mars and Venus*. Oxford: Oxford University Press.

Crystal, D. 1998. *Language Play*. London: Penguin. New edition, 2016, at <http://www.davidcrystal.com>

Crystal, D. 2004. *A Glossary of Netspeak and Textspeak*. Edinburgh: Edinburgh University Press.

Crystal, D. & Crystal, H. 2000. *Words on Words: Quotations about Language and Languages*. London: Penguin. New edition, 2016, at <http://www.davidcrystal.com>

Crystal, D. & Davy, D. 1975. *Advanced Conversational English*. Harlow: Longman.

Du Bois, J. W., Chafe, W. L., Meyer, C., Thompson, S. A., Englebretson, R., & Martey, N. 2000–2005. *Santa Barbara Corpus of Spoken American English, Parts 1–4*. Philadelphia: Linguistic Data Consortium. Available at <https://www.linguistics.ucsb.edu/research/santa-barbara-corpus>

Fletcher, P. 1985. *A Child's Learning of English*. Oxford: Blackwell.

Grice, H. P. 1975. Logic and conversation. In P. Cole & J. Morgan (eds), *Syntax and Semantics*, Vol. 3. New York: Academic Press, 41–58.

James, D. & Clark, S. 1993. Women, men, and interruptions: a critical review. In D. Tannen (ed.), *Oxford Studies in Sociolinguistics: Gender and Conversational Interaction*. New York: Oxford University Press, 231–80.

Kelly, R., O'Malley, M.-P., & Antonijevic, S. 2018. 'Just trying to talk to people . . . It's the hardest': Perspectives of adolescents with high-functioning autism spectrum disorder on their social communication skills. *Child Language Teaching and Therapy*, 34 (3), 319–34.

Malinowski, B. 1923. The problem of meaning in primitive languages. In C. K. Ogden & I. A. Richards, *The Meaning of Meaning*. London: Routledge & Kegan Paul, 296–336.

McTear, M. 1985. *Children's Conversation*. Oxford: Blackwell.

Miller, G. A. 1956. The magic number seven, plus or minus two: some limits on our capacity for processing information. *Psychological Review*, 101 (2), 343–52.

Tomalin, B. & Nicks, M. 2014. *World Business Cultures: A Handbook*, 3rd edition. London: Thorogood Publishing.

Online references

p. vii My website: < http://www.davidcrystal.com>

p. 16 Monty Python sketch: <https://www.youtube.com/watch?v=oa0bCzwSNA0>

p. 131 Hamlet sketch: <https://www.radiotimes.com/news/2016-04-24/prince-charles-joins-benedict-cumberbatch-and-david-tennant-for-superb-hamlet-sketch-at-shakespeare-live/>

p. 185 Hashtag sketch by Foil Arms and Hog (December 2012). <https://www.youtube.com/watch?v=WB2Pp1Scs9k>

p. 185 Hashtag sketch on *The Tonight Show Starring Jimmy Fallon* (24 September 2013). <https://www.youtube.com/watch?list=RD57dzaMaouXA&v=57dzaMaouXA>

p. 187 Use of *LOL*: <http://michelleamcsweeney.com/lol_mcsweeney.pdf>

Some further reading

Miller, S. 2006. *Conversation: a History of a Declining Art.* New York: Yale University Press.

Zeldin, T. 1998. *Conversation: How Talk Can Change Our Lives.* London: Harvill.

Index